WORSHIP
AS PRAISE AND EMPOWERMENT

DAVID R. NEWMAN

———

WORSHIP
as Praise and Empowerment

THE PILGRIM PRESS
New York

Library of Congress Cataloging-in-Publication Data

Newman, David R., 1939–
  Worship as praise and empowerment.
  Bibliography: p. 151.
  1. Public worship. I. Title.
BV15.N49 1988   264   88-2506
        ISBN 0-8298-0774-8 (pbk.)

The Pilgrim Press
132 West 31 Street, New York, NY 10001

Contents

Preface vii

Introduction 1

PART ONE   WHY WORSHIP?

1   Worship in an Age of Power 11
2   The Origin of Worship in the Givenness of Life 21
3   Worship in the New Testament
    as a Celebration of Freedom 36

PART TWO   MODERN OBSTACLES AND NEW POSSIBILITIES

4   Freedom and Authority in Conflict 53
5   The Loss of Transcendence 65
6   The Recovery of Transcendence 79
7   The Power of Metaphor 92

PART THREE   WHAT CAN HAPPEN IN WORSHIP

8   Sunday Morning: Gathering and Sending Forth 107
9   Service of the Word: Proclamation and Response 122
10 The Service of the Table: Honoring Gifts 137

Notes 151

Preface

Worship, when one stops to think about it, is a strange phenomenon. It does not fit easily into the secular worldview of our modern Western society. And yet worship persists, despite various prognostications to the contrary. Indeed the last decade or two have witnessed a surprising upsurge of religious activities. But these have come often as a retreat from full participation in, or encounter with, the dominant forces that shape our age.

The strangeness of Christian worship was the motivating factor for writing this book. Struck by this strangeness I have stopped to wonder and to think about it. And so I have begun with the primary question: "Why worship?" This question has taken me back behind the starting point for most books on worship and liturgy that accept worship as an established fact in its own right. The danger of such a concentration on worship can be a loss of connection between worship and other aspects of life. The way that I have chosen in this book has directed me beyond the discipline of liturgical studies. There is always a risk in interdisciplinary work, but the subject matter of worship in its relation to the whole of life demands such an approach.

My own background of study in philosophy and systematic theology has made me aware of both the pitfalls and the possibilities. In fact, I was first drawn to liturgical studies out of a growing awareness that theological study becomes abstract and highly speculative if it is not grounded in the worship life of a faith community. Liturgy provides a focus for theological inquiry. But this focusing does not constitute a narrowing of the field of study. It is rather, as the movement of the liturgy on Sunday indicates, a gathering and sending forth point for all that we do or think.

In keeping with this view of liturgy and liturgical theology, this book is not the fruit of scholarship pursued in the isolation of a

vii

professor's study. What I have done individually has arisen out of many valuable conversations among people in a wide variety of settings over a number of years. These people include several worshiping congregations, the committee structures of The United Church of Canada, the worship and study environment of Emmanuel College in the ecumenical setting of the Toronto School of Theology, my own personal network of friends within the church and without, and not least, my family, including Nancy, my wife, and our son and daughter, Tom and Ketha. To all these I owe a debt of gratitude.

I would like to thank, in particular, my colleague Prof. Gerald Sheppard at Emmanuel for his invaluable suggestions and encouragement, and Mary Reeve for typing the manuscript.

David R. Newman

Introduction

There is a growing body of literature that accompanies a movement of ecumenical convergence toward renewal of worship in the churches. Much of this writing begins with worship as an accepted fact in the modern churches—a phenomenon that needs no accounting for. Church people may need help in understanding what they are doing when they worship, knowing its history, knowing how, and indeed improving the way they do it. But the fact that they worship needs no explanation. "What happens in worship?" is often asked. But seldom is asked the more basic question: "Why worship?"

That this question "Why?" is not more central in current liturgical study is surely surprising. How quickly times change! Only a few years ago in the secular sixties people were speculating about the possible end of religion in the modern world. Modern secular people, with their growing sense of autonomy and confidence in their own powers, had no need, it was thought, for religion, with all its accoutrements of prayer and worship. Such practices belonged to another era, when people sensed their dependency on powers beyond themselves. What possible place could there be for worship in the new age of power?

The prophecy of the end of religion, as we now know, was at least premature, if not outright wrong. Worship practices still abound in the secular age in possibly more varied ways than ever before. Any writing on the subject needs to acknowledge the plurality of religious practices even when it addresses the concerns of one religious tradition only. Moreover, it is not sufficient to write about worship as if the secular age were now behind us. Our time can still be characterized as an age of power, and people, in even greater measure, as evidenced by the proliferation of liberation movements, are concerned with exercising their own powers.

1

There are also growing anxieties in our time about where the world is going with its newfound powers. Many people are having second thoughts and doubts about the use of their own powers. Besides the liberation movements there are many movements of retrenchment that seek to recover the well-being and security of an earlier era viewed through the mists of fond memory. Some voices cry out for freedom; others, for law and order. Some seek social change; others want to maintain everything as it is. Some expect the worship and outreach of the church to engage with the world in these changes; others want worship to affirm the eternal verities, and hence to enable the church to remain constant in the face of all change. These divergent aims reflect the increasingly sharp polarities of our age.

Where does worship belong in relation to these polarities? Is it edging toward freedom, or serving the existing order? Does it offer hope for change to those who find the social order oppressive, or does it provide comfort and assurance to those who find the way things are to their benefit? Or does worship belong outside these polarities altogether, in a world apart—having to do perhaps more with the next world than with this one, or remaining as a leftover of a bygone era, the end of which has been prematurely pronounced and yet is inevitable? Wherever one stands on these questions the subject of worship is a controversial one in our age. In view of this continuing controversy, the question "Why worship?" remains a pertinent one.

In this book I address this question in the early chapters. The reader will quickly observe that the book does not stay within a narrow range of subject matter defined as "worship." The question "Why?" demands a wider perspective. Worship must be looked at in the context of other movements and activities in society, both past and present. A variety of disciplines are relevant to the study, including anthropology, sociology, philosophy, theology, history, phenomenology, and hermeneutics. Many fine books have been written from one or more of these perspectives. It is a daunting exercise to try to address a question for which all these studies are significant. But it is of the nature of liturgical theology to be integrative of the various disciplines that inquire into human experience. It does this, however, not at the level of constructing an all-embracing system, such as Hegel's philosophy in the last century, which demanded an encyclopedic grasp of knowledge. Few could feel competent enough in all fields for such a task anymore. Rather, it works at the primary level of reflection on experience itself, asking such questions as "Why?" and "What is happening here?" At this level the various disciplines can shed light on the subject without having to be fully represented. Moreover, the analytic approach of these disciplines is not in itself sufficient. If experience is to be viewed as lived and living reality, it must be brought to expression in such a way as to allow the reader to engage with it. For this task, story and metaphor are important in their capacity to evoke an experience by means of the imagination in addition to reflective reasoning. What is lost in precision by this approach is gained by the lively grasp of the subject that is made possible—a grasp that enables the subject to remain alive in its otherness, rather than exist in the abstract only or become a mere object for our inspection. The reader will quickly discern that my method of proceeding includes both storytelling and analysis in what may be called a broad hermeneutical approach. The book, therefore, runs counter to the usual expectations for theological writing, which has customarily proceeded deductively from propositions of faith or definitions, or scientific writing, which analyzes data observed from experience, arriving at conclusions by means of induction.

My approach, which is neither deductive nor inductive, is more akin to the praxis-based method of much current liberation theology—"praxis" being the term used to express a relationship with reality that enables a movement between experience and reflection and back to experience in what has come to be known as a hermeneutical circle. It is a method of exploration that invites the reader on a journey of discovery. For such a journey a map may be helpful to the reader, even though signposts will be erected along the way. The task of mapmaking presupposes knowledge of the destination as well as of the various roads that lead there. For this knowledge to appear in an introduction immediately gives away the fact that the writer, as is often the case, has left the introduction to the last. Reading it first, therefore, is a bit like starting with the last chapter of a novel in order to know the outcome before one begins. Nevertheless, this introduction may be of help to the reader, offering some direction for following the course that the book will be taking.

Chapter 1 with its title "Worship in an Age of Power," begins with a picture of people going to church on a Sunday morning—a most common phenomenon in North American society—in order to pose the question "Why?" It raises the issue of a possible conflict of motivations between worship and the secular attitude of our society. On the one hand, worship begins with an acknowledgment of the "givenness" of life that calls forth an attitude of gratitude and praise. On the other hand, the secular attitude presupposes that human beings are authors of their own destiny and need to be concerned with the uses of the powers at their disposal. Worship would appear, then, to relate more closely to the passivity of life, whereas secularity pertains more to activity—for the former, praise may be due; for the latter, the concern centers on empowerment. The question, with which the chapter ends, gives this book its title: Can worship, rather than falling on one side or the other of this dichotomy, be both praise and empowerment?

Chapter 2 pursues this question by examining more closely the dichotomy of passivity and activity, seeing it as one that runs through the whole of life. Worship, as viewed in primitive experience and in the history of religions, is seen to have its roots in the givenness of life. Religious cults have sought to accommodate themselves to the dichotomy of passivity and activity or mastery by positing a separation of the sacred and the profane. The cult enables the devotee to deal in a separate sacred realm with the powers that, in ordinary life, are not at his or her disposal. But such dealings with the gods are in lieu of exercising responsibility for human destiny in the ordinary course of history. Worship in such cults thus serves to keep human beings passive. An examination of biblical religion, however, reveals a different relationship to the divine powers than occurs in nature cults. The Hebrews and Christians worship a God who acts in history and invites human beings to participate in shaping their own destiny and the destiny of the whole creation. The dichotomy of passivity and activity is thus overcome in a new engagement with the world. But does the freedom and empowerment for this activity entail going beyond

4

ritual practices in a higher spiritual and moral attitude, or is worship in Christian faith transformed to become a ritual or cult of freedom? Chapter 3 examines worship in the New Testament as a celebration of freedom. Christian worship, it is ascertained, continues as a transformed cult that no longer posits the separation of the sacred and profane. The concept of metaphor emerges with reference to worship as a way of understanding how ritual practices can hold together the realities of both the sacred and the profane without losing either. The notion of worship as metaphor is key to subsequent chapters.

Chapter 4 examines the history of worship in the church, which is discerned to be a lapse back into passivity from freedom in a hierarchical structure of authority. This structure once again posits the dualism of the sacred and the profane in a sacramental universe in which all things are held together by an "analogy of being." Philosophy becomes the champion of freedom against the authority of the church. The Enlightenment of the eighteenth century comes as a culminating declaration of freedom against the authority of metaphysics and worship. Atheism emerges as a rejection of the givenness of life in an affirmation of the human capacity for self-making. Does worship rooted in the givenness of life have any place in the secular world after the Enlightenment? Karl Marx, with his call for political revolution, offers an alternative to the worship that has kept people passive in a state of oppression.

Chapters 5 and 6 deal with the question of the loss of transcendence in the modern secular world and with various attempts to recover it up to our own time. Even in the secular era, in which the sense of the sacred has been almost obliterated, there is a dim awareness of the mystery that surrounds the whole of life, and a deep longing to overcome the alienation that afflicts human beings in relation to one another and to the earth itself. These chapters review the various reactions to the loss of faith and transcendence, including romanticism, liberal theology, the ritualism of the high church movement in England, fundamentalism, and movements of social reform that saw worship in instrumental terms or as wholly irrelevant. A new basis for the recovery of transcendence in a secular age as "the beyond in the midst" is found in the work of theologian Dietrich Bonhoeffer. He deals with the dichotomy of passivity and activity by affirming a God who enters our world not in strength, but in the human weakness of the cross of Christ. Christians are called to participate with God in this weakness by living in openness and vulnerability in the world. Worship is the celebration of the coming and presence of God in this new form of transcendence. For this celebration a new language must be learned. This language may be learned in the company of the poor, whose experience of vulnerability is akin to what happened to Jesus on the cross.

Chapter 7, on the power of metaphor, is the culmination of the exploration of the question "Why worship?" Based on a theology of transcendence that overcomes the traditional separation of the sacred and the profane, it picks up once again the concept of metaphor that emerged out of the examination of worship in the New Testament in an earlier chapter. The power of metaphor resides in its capacity to evoke another world. Metaphors can hold together the two realities of the divine and the human, the sacred and the profane, without losing either. As such they can be vehicles of transcendence in our age. Both word and sacraments in worship are best understood, therefore, as metaphors. As metaphors they do not only provide information about one reality or another; they enable participation in the realities of both the human and the divine at once. The power of metaphor is not that of physical force or univocal speech. It is the power of indirection: "this is that" and "this is not that," which always allows reality to remain other and mysterious. Worship celebrates the future God has in store for the world as present even before that future is fully actualized. As a metaphor of the "not yet" in the "now," it has revolutionary power to overturn existing worlds, in the manner of Jesus' parables of the reign of God. In this age of power, when various revolutionary forces are at work, including that of Marxism, worship, too, can be understood as a power for freedom and change in the world. It is a power that, unlike many of the revolutions of our day, keeps life human in the midst of change because life is most human when it acknowledges its source in the creative will of a gracious and loving God. Worship acknowledges this givenness in an act of praise. At the same time, by celebrating God's gift of life as a call into the future God has in store for the world, worship empowers people for living in the world as agents of the love and justice that characterize the reign of God. Worship, therefore, is both praise and empowerment.

The last three chapters move from the question "Why?" to the question "What happens in worship?" It is acknowledged that if the new language of transcendence is to be used in the worship of the churches, some changes will have to come about. Chapter 8 examines the overall movement of worship that combines both gathering and sending, worship and mission. Chapter 9 looks at the Service of the Word in the light of current studies in homiletics. These studies seek to overcome the passivity traditionally associated with preaching by seeing the sermon as a participatory event that engages both the preacher and the people in proclamation and response. The intersection of the text and the situation of the people in the sermon by means of metaphor and story issues in an invitation to enter into the new life of faith in the world in the freedom of the gospel.

Chapter 10 examines the Service of the Table as the place where the people's gifts are honored by being received and transformed into instruments of God's saving action in the world. The Eucharist as communion in the body and blood of Christ is a sign-act or metaphor of the new reality into which God is calling the world in the death and resurrection of Jesus Christ. Christians are called to participate in this reality as a transformed people following their living Savior. To name Jesus as Savior is to take one's cue not from the way things are in the world, but from what God is calling them to be in the world to come. Christians joyfully celebrate the dawning of this new world in their worship even as they strive in their outreach and mission to bring it into being.

In writing this book on worship as praise and empowerment I want to help bring to the fore of liturgical thinking the issue of how the worship of the church relates to its mission of pursuing the justice of God's rule in the world. This concern has come to us most strongly in the theologies of liberation arising out of the struggles of the poor of this world. It is no less a concern for affluent North Americans. We do not see it so clearly perhaps because we have not taken to heart Pogo's insight when he said: "We have met the enemy and he is us." There are many people in our society who are committed to the pursuit of justice but can see in the worship of the churches nothing relevant to their endeavors. To them, it would be good to be able to say that worship *is* concerned about justice and, indeed, that their own efforts, which can become all too grim, can be lightened and enhanced by a worship that keeps life human by celebrating the givenness of life in an act of praise.

The significance of the current reforms of worship cannot, of course, be readily seen by those who have given up on worship, although it may be evident to those who are most active in worship. But we who are involved can become too pleased with our new Service Books and reformed liturgies. To those discouraged with worship, with whom we share a common goal, and to ourselves we need to acknowledge that the reforms have barely begun, and that they will not be realized until the churches can be seen to have entered on a different engagement with the world in which the God, whom we seek to worship, is already fully engaged ahead of us. This outcome of a reformed liturgy, which directs us toward the world and empowers our witness there, will not occur without considerable dislocation and upheaval in the churches. Little of that has yet been experienced. It would be good if we could choose to enter the new time of death and rebirth in a joyful and hopeful spirit. It is in worship that the future God has in store for the world can be glimpsed and celebrated. Without the vision that worship provides, the work that we do gets either misdirected, or carried out under the strict demands of the law rather than in the freedom and the light of the gospel. This book of liturgical theology is inspired by that vision and seeks to serve it.

PART ONE

Why Worship?

1

Worship in an Age of Power

Three people—a man, a woman, and a child—hurry along a nearly deserted city street on a Sunday morning. It is ten to eleven and they have some way yet to walk to the church whose spire can be seen in the distance reaching up among the other buildings that crowd the streetscape. At this time on a Sunday there are not many people about. Some casually dressed people are out for a leisurely stroll, enjoying the holiday air without the usual roar of traffic and smell of exhaust fumes. An occasional jogger weaves in and out among the pedestrians, and there are a few cyclists released from the harassment of negotiating a perilous path through lines of speeding cars. The churchgoers, dressed in their best clothes and in a hurry to go somewhere on a Sunday morning, seem out of place. They are, on this one day, a visible minority in the modern city.

As they walk, one of the three peers into the newspaper dispensers along the sidewalk, trying to catch a glimpse of the headlines in the Sunday papers. On the way home from church they will pick up a paper and enjoy a relaxing brunch while listening to music and reading the news and events of the week and other feature articles. There is a certain predictability in the way the world presents itself each week in the Sunday papers. There may be news items on war in the Middle East, Afghanistan, or Central America. There will be articles that analyze the progress, or lack of it, in the disarmament talks. The uneven distribution of the world's food remains an often-reported concern. People continue to starve in parts of Africa. Of concern also is the continued high rate of unemployment, but society at large seems to have become accustomed to that as a permanent economic con-

11

dition. Other sections of the paper include entertainment, travel, sports, business, classified, and features devoted to such areas as home improvements, physical fitness, and news of general interest having to do, for instance, with the latest fashions or recent discoveries in medicine and health care. The newspaper, in fact, provides a fairly reliable map of the preoccupations of a secular society in the latter part of the twentieth century.

The church spire stands higher as the churchgoers near their destination. The spire, too, is an odd sight amid the other structures along the street. It was meant to stand higher, but in reality it merely holds its own with some of the less impressive neighboring structures. A new high rise nearby nearly dwarfs it. But the high rise does not have a bell. At that very moment the church bell starts ringing, signaling that worship is about to begin. Its deep, resonant sound booms out, wave upon wave, filling the air—not like the usual cacophony of car horns and faulty exhaust systems or the occasional raucous sirens of fire trucks and ambulances. The peal of the bell, out of keeping with modern city sounds, is music to the ears of the churchgoers, who are now approaching the church door. There is a hint of anticipation in the bell, as if it is announcing that something important is about to happen. Even a jogger running by is drawn by the sound, although she continues her set pace unimpeded. There is a moment, though, when she seems to waver slightly in her resolve—an impulse, perhaps like that of Moses, pausing in the desert at the strange sight of a burning bush and taking off his shoes. If she were properly dressed maybe the jogger would stop her run and venture inside the church to see what is happening there.

The three have now reached the church door. Without hesitation they open it and enter. As usual they have cut it very close. This time, in fact, they can hear from the narthex the congregation singing the opening hymn, and they catch a glimpse of the gown of the minister as he enters the sanctuary at the end of the procession. They pause before proceeding in. To hear a crowd of people singing aloud in unison is a cause for wonder even for people who are accustomed to it. To see row upon row of people standing, not before an audience in a concert hall, but directing their chorus simply toward the front of the church, where stands a pulpit with a

Bible on it, a large table, and one or two persons dressed in long white robes, is surely an experience like no other to be ordinarily encountered from day to day. What brings these people here? Who are they singing for, and why? What is going on?

These are some of the questions an observer of such an event would be bound to ask. Anyone might ask them—churchgoer and nonchurchgoer alike. They are also the basic questions of liturgical theology, the subject of this book. A book of liturgical theology does well to begin with the questions anyone can ask. For it is of the very nature of worship to prompt the questions of children and adults, of believers and unbelievers alike. The phenomenon of people gathering together for worship on Sunday morning is the primary datum of liturgical theology.

What happens when Christians gather for worship? This question arises naturally. But it is necessary to ask a more primary question too. Why do Christians worship? This question pertains first to what in experience or faith gives rise to worship. Is reality such that worship is an appropriate response, or does modern experience lead away from worship to other activities that more accurately take account of reality as it is? The first question inquires into causes for worship. A related question asks about the outcome or consequences of worship. What has it to do with what is happening in other areas of life? How does what is happening in church relate to what is going on out on the street and beyond that in the world at large? What has worship to do with the worldly concerns we can read about in the newspapers being sold on the street? These questions about causes and consequences together ask about the relevance of Christian worship.

Before inquiring about what happens in Christian worship we need to consider its relevance because it is by no means self-evident for many people in the present age that Christian worship has any relevance whatever. People demonstrate their indifference to what is going on in the church by not attending worship. Churchgoers are now a minority group in European and North American societies, and there is no reason to think that the group is likely to grow in the years ahead. There is little use in writing about Christian worship without taking this fact into account at the outset.

What accounts for the indifference to the worship of the church in a society where such worship was at one time more central? A pluralistic society offers a multitude of ways of worshiping, to be sure. But even those whose heritage is Christian are falling away from the churches. Is there a growing breach between the motivation for worship and what motivates people for living in society? There is much that can be said on this question about the place of religion and worship in a secular society. I shall begin by noting what appears to be a simple contrast in motivation. It is often pointed out that we live in an age that is preoccupied with achieving results in everything we do. The philosophy that takes this approach to life is called pragmatism, and North Americans are nothing if they are not pragmatic. Furthermore, this primarily Western philosophy is spreading to all parts of the world, particularly through the export of technological products. Modern science has taught us to view the world as a problem to be solved. And our technological achievements have given us confidence in our ability to meet any challenge with a technological solution. The primary preoccupation of our age is the exercise of human power. Before pursuing this thought we need to inquire further about worship.

Worship traditionally has had less to do with the exercise of human power than with the recognition of the limits to that power. In the face of such occurrences as birth, death, accident, and disease, over which they have had little or no control, human beings have come to accept a certain givenness to life. The primary force behind the whole of life is seen to be not in human beings, but in God. Worship is an act of praise, of ascribing worth to God, the Giver of life, as the derivation of the word worship, from the Anglo-Saxon "worthship," would indicate. This praise of an all-powerful deity has often occurred as an act of abasement on the part of human beings. True devotion has required acknowledgment and acceptance of our passivity before almighty God.

Many worship practices would appear to confirm the worshipers in their passivity. In a typical Protestant or Catholic worship service the sheer inactivity of the congregation as, for the most part, they sit in rows of pews listening to readings, sermons, and prayers would seem inevitably to impart a passive attitude. The widely

14

held expectation that worship ought to provide a refuge from the busy world, a respite from the rapid pace of change, does nothing to diminish the passivity of the worshiper. This no doubt accounts also for the antique air that pervades many churches whose primary association is with the past century. The market for discarded church furnishings underlines this antique quality and at the same time brings some buyers as close to the worship of their forebears as they are likely to get. In churches known for their more vigorous approach to worship the people sing and shout, clap their hands, and dance in the aisles but may be no less passive than those in the more decorous environment of the mainline churches. All this activity also may be an appealing retreat from active engagement with the contemporary world into the comforting security of "old-time religion." The exercise of authority, moreover, in informal worship settings often surpasses that of more formal liturgy in the psychological hold the leader maintains over the congregation.

There is, however, a virtual consensus among liturgical reformers of most denominations that the people ought to participate fully in both the worship and the outreach of the church. The impetus for this reform is coming from a variety of sources, including the recovery of early, more authentic practices of Christian worship. But more directly it is being called for by the people themselves who, in increasing numbers, are seeking to assume more responsibility for their own lives as Christians. This struggle for freedom against inherited structures of authority, although it is espoused as yet by only a minority, can be regarded as one of the liberation movements of our time. At the same time, however, the churches are all experiencing resistance to this reform. This resistance may arise partly out of the difficulty people have in changing deeply ingrained habits; it may point to shortcomings in the education that accompanies the worship and mission, or to ineffectual leadership. But it may be more deeply rooted in the motivations we have begun to explore that place worship on the passive side of life. Worship regarded as passivity would lead some to seek it as a respite from the worldly activities that are their main preoccupations in life. Others would reject worship on these grounds as being irrelevant to the church's mission. If a reform of worship is to occur that empowers people for living an active life in the world, it will be necessary to inquire more closely into this pattern of passivity and activity within which we have begun to view worship.

The pattern of passivity and activity can be seen to run through the whole of life. It appears in the familiar dichotomies of law and freedom, powerlessness and power, weakness and strength. In our Western patriarchal tradition, where mainly "male" attributes are applied to God, the pattern assumes the form of a hierarchy of creator and creature, father and child (and wife), master and slave. In the goddess religion of a matriarchal society it will be seen more in relation to forces of nature that determine also human life and to which human beings have to accommodate themselves. And, of course, these societies also have the master-slave relationship. This dichotomy of passivity and activity will be examined in chapter 2.

Our own age, which can be characterized as an age of power, understandably has serious difficulty with any awareness of the givenness of life and the dichotomy of passivity and activity as a description of the whole of life. If anything, though, it has sharpened the dichotomy into one of either passivity or mastery. In this sharply polarized situation the association of religion and worship with an awareness of the givenness of life and its accompanying sense of passivity makes these "activities" a questionable option for people engaged in a struggle for power. Where human beings have become increasingly aware of the implications for all life of the exercise of their own power for good or ill, accepting passivity appears as a threat to the full realization of life. Worship that arises out of the sense of passivity as a response to the givenness of life can be seen as standing in the way of human responsibility for the use of power. Do the traditionally powerless groups in society, including the poor, women, blacks, native people, and other oppressed minorities, who have always sensed their existence as being owed to another, have to reject religion and worship as a way of breaking out of their passivity, now experienced as bondage? And conversely does not a religion of passivity offer the powerful a useful means of sanctioning their position in relation to the powerless?

The uses of power have always been a pressing concern. In a world where these uses have come even more to the fore, religion and worship rooted in the passivity of life appear to be, at best, irrelevant to the major issues facing humanity and, at worst, a barrier to dealing with them. People are becoming aware as perhaps never before of the almost unimaginable powers at the disposal of human beings through the exercise of technology. The most pervasive power is clearly nuclear, with the specter it raises of the possible annihilation of life on earth. Reaching out to the stars is another, extending the scope of human existence into areas that at one time were believed to be the abodes of the gods. The use of computer and robot technology in communication and manufacture promises an enrichment of life in the areas of knowledge and personal living style that is beyond anything the world has previously known. In the field of genetics the prospect before us is of an evolution of which humankind is no longer a product, but an agent with the power, through the exercise of genetic control, of shaping the future of all living creatures, including human beings.

To the view that this age can be characterized by the extent of its use of power might be countered the view that humankind has also had to come to terms most sharply with the limits of its power. People in no other age have had it quite so forcefully put to them that their own era might be the last because of their own abuse of power. So powerful has been the impact on our imaginations of the threat of global catastrophe in a nuclear holocaust that the mushroom cloud has become a primary symbol of our age. People date this age from the fateful day in the summer of 1945 when such a cloud first appeared over an American desert in an experiment code-named Trinity. J. Robert Oppenheimer, one of the scientists responsible for the explosion, reported later that at the sight of the huge ball of fire and cloud he thought of the words of the God Krishna in the Hindu scriptures, *The Bhagavadgita:* "I am become death, the shatterer of worlds." But even the looming prospect of an imminent self-inflicted end to all life on earth in a nuclear winter does not attest to the limits of human power. Suicide is an ultimate way of taking life into one's own hands, and therefore a perverse exercise of power.

But perhaps in another way human beings in this age have become conscious of the limits of their power. Beside the horror of the mushroom cloud, another symbol has come to grip the imaginations of people in the twentieth century. This symbol attests not to the hideous outcome of an earth laid waste by a perverse use of human power, but to the stunning beauty of a planet whose mysterious origin lies outside the range of all human willing and doing. On one voyage, as part of an all-out American effort to place the first human being on the moon ahead of the Russians, an American astronaut idly turned his gaze away from the object of his endeavor to take a picture of Earth, which was gradually receding behind him. The photograph of the Blue Planet floating like a jewel in space immediately caught the imaginations of people everywhere. It called forth a new awareness of how precious is our planet in the vast universe and of our need for solidarity as human beings with one another and with all living creatures who share this "island home." The achievement of getting to the moon first—no doubt one of the greatest enterprises in human history—may have attested, as intended, to the superiority of American technology and even to the whole American way of life. But it was eclipsed by a symbol that emerged from the enterprise, not as an intended outcome of the technology, but as a mere accidental by-product. The symbol of the Blue Planet will remain in an age of power as a reminder to human beings of the limits of that power and a witness to the ultimate givenness of life that is forever a cause of wonder.

Is there a place, then, for worship in an age of power when worship has been closely associated with the experience of powerlessness? The religious tendency to equate sin with weaknesses in human nature does not address the evil and alienation that arise from human strength. The association of goodness with passivity, often thought to be a special grace of women, stands in the way of people's desire, as women have ruefully found, for the betterment of conditions in their own lives and the lives of others. Can people continue to worship in good conscience and invite others to join them when the powerful of this world have so often urged worship on the powerless to keep them there? President Ronald Reagan announced that he was going to put God back into the classrooms of America. Even God is at the disposal of the rulers of this world. Are we to worship such a God? Is all worship but a service of civil religion, with its sacred festivals honoring the powerful of this world? Has it no other end than that of confirming the alienation of the status quo, as Karl Marx asserted? In the image of the Blue Planet we possibly get a hint of something different in that people can serve a greater end than that of our private and patriotic strivings—an end that unites all human beings in a shared joy and a shared responsibility because it is not only a product of our own willing and doing, but also a response to something given. In this acknowledgment of the givenness of life still may reside the possibility of genuine worship.

A major concern of Christians in our age has to be the struggle for an authentic expression of worship that liberates and empowers people to act responsibly rather than enslaving them, that overcomes alienation rather than confirming it. Worship as praise only can exalt God at the expense of human beings, thereby diminishing their responsibility for their own lives. It seeks a sphere of human existence that is untouched by, and thereby acquiescing in, the dominant forces at work in human society. The voices that are crying out for justice not only in society at large, but in the church itself, are left unheard. Worship ought also to empower. But worship as empowerment only, without praise, is put at the service of individual need as a private indulgence, something to get by on but only useful while the need remains. Or it loses itself in the cause of particular conflicting movements in society, pursuing this end and that, but always fashioning a god only to serve whatever ends are in view. A god that is put at our human disposal is always an idol. Worship, therefore, must include both praise and empowerment.

Is there not, then, an appropriate acknowledgment of the givenness of life—an acknowledgment that reins in the power of those who seek to hold all power unto themselves? Is worship not, above all, a way of letting God be God over against any who would seek to be gods? There is a perplexity in the experience of worship in an age of power that needs to be addressed. The perplexity pertains to the issues of powerlessness and power that we have begun to consider.

How can worship offer both praise and empowerment? Is there a worship that in offering praise to a God who is beyond the powers of this world calls this world's powers into question—that in acknowledging the givenness of life, and thereby not seeking mastery in the competition of worldly powers, subverts these powers

19

and offers genuine freedom? These are the questions this book seeks to address. They will take us farther along the path of inquiry into the origin and outcome of Christian worship before we attempt to look at what happens in Christian worship by examining the liturgy that Christians engage in on Sunday mornings. In the next chapter I shall explore the passivity that underlies many religious practices and raise the question whether in Christian worship, as a response to the givenness of life, this dichotomy of passivity and activity or mastery can be overcome.

2

The Origin of Worship in the Givenness of Life

In the novel *Island* Aldous Huxley depicts a society in which love, peace, and harmony reign. It is an island paradise based on the philosophy and religious practices of the East, existing in an alienated and war-torn world in which the scientific outlook prevails and the power of technology rules. A journalist from the outside world visits the island and is introduced to many of its ways. One day he shares a meal at the home of one of the island families. Before they sit down to eat, the grace is explained to him. Not a word will be spoken for a space of time. Each one takes a morsel of food and begins to chew, savoring its qualities, its blend of flavors, its texture. Grace is a silent rumination on the essential goodness of the food.

When the visitor asks, "And meanwhile, I suppose, you give thanks to the Enlightened One, or Shiva, or whoever it may be?" the answer comes, "That would distract your attention, and attention is the whole point. Attention to the experience of something given, something you haven't invented, not the memory of a form of words addressed to somebody in your imagination."[1]

The visitor reflects in his question another kind of grace: "Blessed is the Lord our God, Maker of the Universe, who causes bread to come forth from the earth." Here, too, there is gratitude for something given. But instead of silence, words are spoken, indeed words that echo in memory down through the generations. Attention, moreover, is focused not only on the goodness of what is given, but also toward the goodness of the Giver in an act of praise. These words are from the *Kiddush*, an ancient mealtime grace of the Jews. It was a prayer known to Jesus and said by him at meals with his friends. Christians are familiar with this way of praying from the meal Jesus had with his disciples in the Upper Room before his crucifixion. They continue so to pray in the Eucharist, the service of praise and thanksgiving in word and sacrament, which is at the heart of all Christian worship.

Here are two ways of worship. Their differences can be easily discerned. One happens in silence. In the other the silence is broken by words. In one, language is thought to get in the way of the reality experienced. In the other, language is a means of communicating with the reality behind what is experienced. Attention, therefore, in one rests on what is given. In the other, it is directed to the Giver. They are two ways of worship, but in both there is a grateful awareness of something given. Food, that most basic requirement of life, is the occasion for the gratitude. In the acknowledgment that food is given one can discern an awareness of the givenness of the whole of life. This awareness of the givenness of life is the root from which religion and worship grow.

The religious consciousness is grounded in the experience of "existence owed to another."[2] The countervailing view, particularly prevalent in modern technological society, is that existence is of one's own making. Together they form a dichotomy running through the whole of life that may be expressed also as passivity and activity. The two belong together—sometimes existing in harmony and at other times one predominating over the other.

Passivity is sensed in many ways: in being born; in the helplessness of infancy; in aging, accident, and disease; in the experience of hunger; and in the inevitability of death. It comes also in the touch of another, a sound that startles, or a fragrance that gradually insinuates itself on the senses. It is being aware of otherness. Sometimes this otherness fades from our awareness as we become more conscious of our own activity of experiencing or using. Then our activity predominates over passivity. We encounter the other only as an object at our own disposal.

In different societies the dichotomy of passivity and activity occurs in different ways. In a primitive agrarian society passivity is experienced in the uncertainty of the weather, in the change of seasons, in the mystery of growth and decay. Beside these are the activities of planting and tilling and harvest, and the ability to create, in toolmaking, building shelter, and the arts and crafts. The dichotomy between passivity and activity in the natural environment can become a harmony. But sometimes the harmony is broken by aggressive human activity or by the disruptive forces of the natural elements of sun, wind, and water. When these natural forces prevail, humankind experiences a profound sense of passivity.

In the primitive hunting society human activity assumes the more aggressive form of seeking mastery. With the weapons they devise the hunters are able to attain a position of superiority even over the most ferocious of wild animals. But the sense of passivity is present even when the sense of mastery seems to predominate. The hunters are not without awareness during the hunt that life is not entirely of their own making. It is sensed in the contingency of whether or not the hunt will be successful, but perhaps most strongly at the moment of triumph when the hunters gaze into the terror-filled eyes of the stricken animals and see not only the death of the hunted, but the fear of their own death reflected there. The hunters, too, are the hunted!

In William Golding's novel *Lord of the Flies* a group of schoolboys find themselves alone on a deserted island after a plane crash. The situation at first is like a game to them. But soon their carefree existence is threatened, not by external danger, but by their own fears and desires. Their innocent pastimes gradually change until what they do takes on all the features of a primitive society. They become a tribe of hunters complete with painted masks to ward off evil spirits, tribal dances to stir up their lust for blood, and sacrifices to placate a god of their imagining.

While on a hunt one day in the forest one of the boys, who became the leader of the hunters, unwittingly reveals what lay behind this momentous change: "If you're hunting," he says, "sometimes you catch yourself feeling as if"—and here he pauses—"there's nothing in it of course. Just a feeling. But you can feel as if you're not hunting, but being hunted; as if something's behind you all the time in the jungle."[3]

The pattern of life that includes both passivity and mastery is depicted in the biblical account in Genesis of the creation and fall of our human progenitors. God has given Adam and Eve the freedom of the garden in which to live in peace and harmony. In the center of the garden are the tree of life and the tree of knowledge of good and evil. Only the tree of knowledge of good and evil, the fruit of which it is forbidden for them to eat, is out of bounds. They can have their freedom only in accepting this limit. The limit at the center of life, represented by the forbidden tree, is the incontrovertible fact that the Source and Origin of their lives are outside themselves and therefore not at their disposal.[4]

But the parents of the human race do not accept such a limit. They want to have their lives at their own disposal. And so they eat. The tranquility of the garden is disrupted by their disobedience. Where before the garden was a home for them, it now becomes a hiding place from the accusing presence of God. They seek to evade God's question: "Where are you?" This question in the midst of human attempts to make our own lives is a constant reminder that life is not at our disposal. We owe it to another.

In the Bible this imagery of God the hunter is transformed into that of a shepherd looking after a flock, as in Psalm 23, and going out to find the sheep when they are lost, as in the imagery of the good shepherd that is applied to Jesus. The question "Where are you?" therefore, is one that can induce both fear and gratitude. Our response to the givenness of life is an uneasy mixture of both fear and gratitude before what has been called the "uncanny"[5] or, in Rudolf Otto's phrase, the *mysterium tremendum et fascinans*.[6] The worshiper is both repelled and enticed and so is filled, in the words of the hymn writer, with "wonder, love, and praise."[7] The image of sheep and shepherd is an image of hierarchy and power. Little sheep never grow up to be shepherds. But even this power image is transformed in the Bible as the shepherd becomes the lamb that is slain, offering us a glimpse of the mysterious way in which the dichotomy of passivity and activity can be overcome.

The history of religions reveals diverse ways of dealing with this dichotomy of passivity and activity. The sense of passivity has possibly been most completely expressed in the concept of taboo, which in the Polynesian islands, where the term originated, stands for religion itself. Taboo stands for all the unknown powers to which human life is subject. The taboo system provides a means of dealing with the dangers these powers impose on human life. The innumerable restrictions pertaining to what had to be avoided or abstained from often became an intolerable burden, but at the same time it provided, as Ernst Cassirer has noted, a "system of social restriction and obligation" that is basic to life in society.[8]

The related notion of magic appears to involve a more positive and active approach to the unknown powers. Instead of merely submitting to the mysterious forces of nature, magic seeks to put them to use and thereby to exercise some control. This exercise of control in magical practice involves elaborate rituals that have to be performed according to a strict order if the right effect is to be produced. The intense concentration that this requires shows a developing sense of confidence on the part of human beings in their own power. With its use of the powers at its disposal, magic has been called a primitive technology.

Whether taboo or magic, as responses to the passivity of life, can be regarded as expressions of worship is difficult to establish. The relationship between magic and religion has remained unclear to religious anthropologists, although some connection is generally assumed. Few, however, would agree with James G. Frazer, who asserts in *The Golden Bough* that magic is a prior stage that human beings have to go through before they arrive at the religious stage where they recognize their total dependence on the mysterious divine powers now conceived of in personal terms.[9] Such submission cannot, at least from the modern perspective, be regarded as an advance on what magic purports to do. Nor does the concept of total dependence necessarily provide an adequate perception of what religion in all its forms can be, despite its obvious connection with passivity. There are, moreover, magical elements that coexist with many religious practices. In ritual sacrifice people have sought to please and placate the gods and so to influence how their lives are disposed of. The insistence in the rituals of many religions on a strict adherence to an intricate set of rules and a prescribed order so as to ensure the desired effects has a clear affinity with magic.

Mircea Eliade describes the sense of passivity in archaic religion as a "terror of history."[10] The cult provides a way of coping with this terror through "the myth of the eternal return." This myth, which is associated with the cyclical forces of birth, death, and rebirth in nature, affirms the possibility of returning again and again to the time of origin and thereby renewing failing powers. Within this religious consciousness there is no sense of history as an arena of human activity in which the will and purpose of human beings have some effect on shaping their futures. For dealing with life's crises, such as illness, crop failure, or enemy attack, the individual and tribe primarily rely, not on their own remedial action, but on the ritual of the cult. The empowerment that comes through the imitation of archetypes and paradigmatic gestures of the cult is, therefore, in lieu of the responsibility of human beings for working out their own destiny. The cult provides a means, as Eliade says, of escape from history.

The ancient Hebrews came to quite a different assessment of the significance of human involvement in worldly happenings. A shift took place from a passive to an active role in shaping history, arising out of a changed perception of the powers that transcend human life. Gerhard von Rad has noted that the distinctiveness of biblical religion in relation to the other religions of the ancient East can be discerned in the Hebrew prohibition against the use of images in worship, found in the second commandment of the Decalogue (Deuteronomy 27:15, Exodus 20:4). He has written:

Without any doubt the inhabitant of the ancient East was confronted in his physical environment by the deity in a much more immediate way than Israel could say that Jahweh confronted her. In the greater and lesser religions of the ancient East the gods were personified powers of heaven or earth or the abyss. But this was not the way in which Jahweh was related to the world. However powerful his sway in it was, theologically he still transcended it. Nature was not a mode of Jahweh's being; he stood over against it as its Creator. This then means that the commandment forbidding images is bound up with the hidden way in which Jahweh's revelation came about in cult and history.[11]

To make an image of God is to take away God's freedom—to have a god at one's own disposal. The Hebrews rejected the nature cults and their images in favor of *YHWH*, a creator God, by whose action the world of nature and history comes into being. This God, who cannot be identified with the elemental powers in nature and the cosmos, is free to encounter and be encountered by human beings in the events that make up their history. Human beings, in turn, are called to participate with God in shaping the course of history. History has, therefore, become for both God and human beings the place and mode of their common presence and activity. In this history the separation of the sacred from the profane that characterizes most religions does not pertain. There is no need for sacred precincts and seasons because any place and any time can be an epiphany of the Deity. Human life is fulfilled not by appeal to the will of the gods in ritual sacrifice, but by responding to God's presence in the ordinary course of daily life.

The decisive event in Israel's history, wherein the action of God was discerned, was the Hebrews' deliverance from slavery in Egypt. This belief in God's action in history enabled the Hebrews to find meaning and value in the events that befell Israel, whether historical catastrophes or national successes, instead of seeking an escape from history in a myth of the eternal return. Of this development Eliade has written:

> For the first time, we find affirmed, and increasingly accepted, the idea that historical events have a value in themselves, insofar as they are determined by the will of God. . . . It may then be said with truth that the Hebrews were the first to discern the meaning of history as the epiphany of God and this conception, as we should expect, was taken up and amplified by Christianity.[12]

This discovery of the "irreversibility of time" and the "new"[13] in history, according to Eliade, is Israel's great achievement in the history of religion. It had a decisive effect on Israel's worship.

In place of the contemporaneousness of the nature cult, the once-and-for-all quality of God's saving acts was affirmed. The traditional nature festivals of Canaanite religion were historicized by Israel to refer to God's deliverance of the Hebrews from Egypt and the giving of the covenant. Worship was now a rehearsal of God's mighty acts in history in an act of praise. This praise was not offered, as were the traditional sacrifices, for the purpose of placating God or winning some influence with the divine that would produce an increase in one's own power. It was a sign of Israel's love for God. Even this love was not understood in immanental terms as a natural affinity with or affection for God. It was a response to God's commandment to love, as we see in the Shema, which is repeated to this day by Jews in both home and synagogue. "Hear [Shema], O Israel: The Lord our God is one Lord; and you shall love the Lord your God with all your heart, and with all your soul, and with all your might [Deut. 6:4–5]."

This commandment to love is a basis not only for praise, but also for empowerment because it is the motive behind the way the people are to act in their daily lives, especially toward those who are in need: "[God] executes justice for the fatherless and the widow, and loves the sojourner, giving him food and clothing. Love the sojourner therefore; for you were sojourners in the land of Egypt [Deut. 10:18–19]." The "therefore" in this text is especially to be noticed. God has loved you, *therefore*. . . . The people of Israel are to love because they have been loved. This love is the link between their worship and their concern for justice. Far from diminishing human responsibility for shaping history, as happened in the ritual of the cult, the worship of *YHWH* renews the commitment of the worshiper to an active participation in fulfilling God's loving intention in the world.

We see in the prophetic criticism of the worship of Israel, however, that it was susceptible to losing its connection with responsible action in history by confining God's action to a past that could be recovered only in the timeless repetitions of the cult. Worship as referring only to the past loses sight of God's actions in the present. Worship becomes separated from a continuing history of God's dealing with humankind. With this separation comes also a loss of concern for God's justice.

> Fasting like yours this day
>   will not make your voice to be heard
>   on high.
> Is such the fast that I choose,
>   a day for a man to humble himself?
> Is it to bow down his head like a rush,
>   and to spread sackcloth and ashes
>   under him?
> Will you call this a fast,
>   and a day acceptable to the Lord?
> Is not this the fast that I choose:
>   to loose the bonds of wickedness,

to undo the thongs of the yoke,
to let the oppressed go free,
and to break every yoke?
Is it not to share your bread with the
hungry,
and bring the homeless poor into
your house;
when you see the naked, to cover him,
and not to hide yourself from your
own flesh?
Then shall your light break forth like
the dawn,
and your healing shall spring up
speedily.   —Isaiah 58:4–8

God is not pleased with praise that goes no farther than an attitude of passive abasement. Genuine worship issues in action in the present according to God's will for justice in the world.

In contrast to the tendency to remove worship from current history, the prophets had an unprecedented awareness of God's action in the events of their own day. They expected, moreover, a *new* action of *YHWH*, soon to happen, that would be decisive for the whole of Israel's existence. God's salvation of the people could not be confined to events in the historical past remembered in the cult. Salvation was now ahead of them. There would be a new entry into the land (Hosea), a new David and a new Zion (Isaiah), a new covenant (Jeremiah), and a new Exodus (Deutero-Isaiah). This expectation of God's action in the present and immediate future that corresponds with God's actions in the past can be called "eschatological," if that term is not reserved for the cosmic catastrophe that ends all history (the eschaton). The prophets had no such absolute understanding of an end of history. It was only later that Persian apocalyptic notions were melded with the prophetic expectation giving rise to the belief that history would be abolished, even more decisively than in the earlier cosmogonic outlook, in a final event that puts a definitive end to history.[14]

God's action is celebrated by the Hebrews not only with reference to the past and present. Informed by the eschatological outlook of the prophets, the Hebrews celebrated also in their

29

worship a future when righteousness will prevail and the land will be restored to fruitfulness.

> Steadfast love and faithfulness will meet;
>   righteousness and peace will kiss each other.
> Faithfulness will spring up from the ground,
>   and righteousness will look down
>   from the sky.
> Yea, the Lord will give what is good,
>   and our land will yield its increase.
> Righteousness will go before him,
>   and make his footsteps a way. —Psalm 85:10–13

This future can be looked forward to as a gift from God, but not as an alternative to the people's striving for righteousness and peace. The givenness that pertains to the future is to be perceived as an openness to enter upon the way that leads to what is promised. According to the Bible, the Israelites understood themselves to be pilgrims on the way to the Promised Land.

Christianity emerged within this Israelite perspective that re-directed the worshiper toward the world. The apocalyptic outlook, with its expectation of an imminent end of history, was current at the time of Jesus and informed his preaching of the coming of the kingdom of God. It was also a view shared by the apostle Paul. But Christian faith altered the apocalyptic expectation by affirming that, in some preliminary way, the end had already broken into history in the coming of Jesus as the expected Messiah. God's decisive entry into history in Jesus, the Messiah or Christ, moves Christians to make a full affirmation of history over against any religious tendencies to withdraw into a separate sphere.

The cross of Christ is a sign for Christians of God's entry into history, not with insuperable power, but in the vulnerability of suffering. The faithful, who see themselves as the body of Christ, are called to enter into this vulnerability as in a "fellowship of his sufferings" (Philippians 3:10). The resurrection of Christ is a sign that the cross is not only a noble way to die—as, for instance, Socrates' drinking of the cup of hemlock—but also a way to live a life characterized by love. Here passivity, as seen in the passion of Christ on the cross, becomes not a sign of abject submission to the powers that be, but, paradoxically, a sign of the victory of love over them. This victory is revealed in the resurrection. To the one who accepts the vulnerability of the cross the resurrection says: "You have a future." It is a future that Christians believe God intends for the whole world.

The response in Christian worship to the givenness of life includes not only gratitude for God's saving actions in the past, therefore, but also openness to the future God has in store for the whole world. In his book *The Church, Change and Development*, Ivan Illich has spoken of the future orientation of Christian worship in a striking fashion:

The future has already broken into the present. We each live in many times. The present of one is the past of another, and the future of yet another. We are called to live knowing that the future exists, and that it is shared when it is celebrated. [15]

Christian worship incorporates into itself the Hebrew transformation of ritual from a timeless rite that escapes history to a rehearsal of God's saving acts in the past and prophetic anticipation of the future. Both past and future are present to the worshiper in remembrance and hope. The Bible ends with a vision of the culmination of all things in which past and future come together in an act of worship that continues throughout eternity.

After this I heard what seemed to be the loud voice of a great multitude in heaven, crying,
"Hallelujah! Salvation and glory and
    power belong to our God,
for his judgments are true and just; . . ."
And the twenty-four elders and the four living creatures fell down and worshiped God who is seated on the throne, saying, "Amen. Hallelujah!"
And from the throne came a voice crying,
"Praise our God, all you his servants,
you who fear him, small and great."
Then I heard what seemed to be the voice of a great multitude, like the sound of many waters and like the sound of mighty thunderpeals, crying,
"Hallelujah! For the Lord our God the
    Almighty reigns.
Let us rejoice and exult and give him
    the glory. . . ."   —Revelation 19:1–2a, 4–7a

This picture of worship in Revelation 19 as eternal praise of a God enthroned on high would appear, however, to be an absolutizing of the hierarchical master-slave relationships that exist within a patriarchal society. Northrop Frye, in his examination of biblical metaphor in *The Great Code: The Bible and Literature*, affirms this understanding of the apocalyptic vision of worship but maintains that worship itself is finally transcended in a "participatory" vision that goes beyond the dichotomies of the legal realm. He distinguishes two apocalyptic visions in the book of Revelation. The first is what he calls a "panoramic apocalypse," in which the legal metaphor still pertains of final judgment, heaven and hell, prosecution and defense, and humankind "eternally a creature, praising his Creator unendingly."[16] But this panoramic apocalypse

gives way, at the end, to a second apocalypse that, ideally, begins in the reader's mind as soon as he has finished reading, a vision that passes through the legalized vision of ordeals and trials and judgments and comes out in a second life. In this second life the creator-creature, divine-human antithetical tension has ceased to exist, and the sense of the transcendent person and the split of subject and object no longer limit our vision. After the "last judgment," the law loses its last hold on us, which is the hold of the legal vision that ends there.[17]

Professor Frye's affirmation of a final vision in the book of Revelation that transcends ritual worship in a higher spiritual or moral attitude brings the Bible close to a religious attitude, or attitude toward religion, that can be found in various manifestations in both East and West. In the West it has appeared in such varying phenomena as the great mystical tradition, movements of iconoclasm, the intellectual tradition of philosophy, and the ethical and political movements in the modern era for betterment of the human condition. In the East it appears as the ultimate goal of religion in enlightenment, the *samadhi* of Hinduism or the *satori* of Zen. For example, Radhakrishnan, in his commentary on the Hindu sacred text, *The Bhagavadgita*, states that "name and form are used to reach the Formless,"[18] but "for those of illuminated consciousness, ritual observances are of little value."[19] With reference to the Vedic rituals, the text itself says:

As is the use of a pond in a place flooded with water everywhere,
So is that of all the Vedas for the Brahmin who understands.[20]

Influenced by Eastern religions, Aldous Huxley depicted the worship of his mythical island as without ritual in contrast with the expectations of the visiting Western journalist. In his account the difference is expressed in terms of attention being addressed directly to what is given in life instead of toward the Giver. It is this latter indirect response to the givenness of life that occasions the use of words and ritual actions in worship. From Frye's account we could conclude that such worship remains always within the legal realm, in contrast with a higher spiritual attitude that is more immediate and characterized by freedom instead of law.

What is at issue here is decisive for our examination of liturgy as praise and empowerment. Does Christian worship belong only to a penultimate realm of law where such institutions as marriage, government, and church, and the rhythms of the natural order pertain? Or is it an expression of a different kind of relationship described as gospel, which is the distinctive category applied to the life of faith in the New Testament? If the former is the case, there will be no other possibility for empowerment in worship than what we have seen within the dichotomy of passivity and mastery. With its rootedness in the passivity of life the cult can offer no more than an illusory empowerment in a separate sphere, apart from the realm of human activity in history. But we have already observed in the Bible a challenge to the separation of cult from history and an affirmation of worship as renewing the worshiper's commitment to historical existence and God's call for justice in relationships among human beings and toward nature. If worship resides only within the realm of law, the kind of empowerment it can offer can be no more than what comes from the power of law to enforce conformity with its precepts or, as in the nature cult, conformity with the elemental forces of nature. This is clearly a relationship of subordination to a higher authority or power. It is the opposite of the kind of empowerment that issues in freedom.

In the gospel, however, as Karl Barth has pointed out, the law is transformed from being what one ought to conform to, to what one *may* or indeed *can* realize in one's own life, empowered by the Spirit. God's commandment is "permission."[21] The Jewish understanding of Torah contains a similar transformation of the ordinary perception of law into a law that is at the root of freedom rather than being opposed to it. "When Torah entered the world, freedom entered it," the Jewish worshiper affirms.[22] As such it is a law that can be described as grace. For this reason the Hebrew Bible and worship are full of expressions of praise to God for giving Israel the Torah. In Hebrew eschatology the Torah will never pass away, as this prayer in praise of the Torah, after it is read in the synagogue, indicates:

> Blessed is the Lord our God, Ruler of the universe,
>   who has given us a Torah of truth,
>   implanting within us eternal life.
> Blessed is the Lord, Giver of the Torah.[23]

As long as there is Torah there will be worship in praise of Torah. Can the same affirmation be made of Christian worship as it is depicted in the book of Revelation, or does the gospel and the faith it elicits transcend worship?

In the book of Revelation the legal sphere is indeed depicted as coming to an end. But worship appears to remain after all the institutions of the legal realm, including "church," have ceased to exist. Worship is the lasting metaphor for the true and perfect, and hence transformed, relationship between creature and Creator.

In the final vision there is "a new heaven and a new earth; for the first heaven and the first earth had passed away [Rev. 21:1]." In the holy city, the new Jerusalem, God "dwells with" humankind and they are "his people [v. 3]." There is no longer the rhythm of day and night or the seasons of the year, for the sun and moon are replaced by the light of God's countenance. There is no sacrificial worship as a means of reconciling humanity and God: there is "no temple in the city, for its temple is the Lord God the Almighty and the Lamb [v. 22]." There will no longer be a day of worship because every day is filled with worship; nor will there be a sacred place for worship because every space is sanctified:

But the throne of God and of the Lamb shall be in it, and his servants shall worship him; they shall see his face, and his name shall be on their foreheads. And night shall be no more; they need no light of lamp or sun, for the Lord God will be their light, *and they shall reign for ever and ever.* (Rev. 22:3–5, emphasis added)

Worship continues, but something remarkable has happened to it. The order of worship is no longer a hierarchy of a servant bowing to a master. The servant has become a sovereign ruling over everything. Worship as metaphor for gospel is transformed

34

from service into sovereign freedom, from work into play. It is the "eschatological game"[24] in which the saved and reconciled community live out their relationship with the God who no longer rules over them, but "dwells with" them. There is no dichotomy between praise and empowerment. Praise is now the acknowledgment of the origin of freedom and, therefore, the source of the empowerment that flows from worship. Worship is a celebration of freedom.

There is in the final vision a "river of the water of life" and a "tree of life" yielding its fruit in all seasons. These do not come to an end. The church has identified them respectively with the water of Baptism and the bread and wine of the Eucharist. Baptism is the entrance to the common meal that will be celebrated in eternity: "Blessed are those who wash their robes, that they may have the right to the tree of life and that they may enter the city by the gates [Rev. 22:14]."

What remains to be considered is how closely this apocalyptic vision of worship in eternity resembles the actual worship of the church in a world where the legal realm still remains. This is not a question of whether the writer of the book of Revelation was depicting heavenly worship or a model of worship as actually practiced in the churches with which he was familiar at the time of writing. Although there are discernible elements of actual worship in the seer's vision, no direct correspondence can likely be drawn between the ritual in heaven and any worship services in the early Christian communities.[25] My question rather is regarding the freedom of the gospel as expressed in the vision of heavenly worship and whether that freedom characterizes also the worship of the church. I want now to examine the practice of worship in the New Testament with a view to assessing its freedom.

3

Worship in the New Testament as a Celebration of Freedom

In the apocalyptic vision of the book of Revelation worship is depicted as an action of the freedom of the gospel after the legal realm has passed away. The temple, holy days, and sacral priests have ceased to be. But worship remains as a metaphor for the sanctification of the whole of life. How is this vision of worship in eternity to be understood in relation to the historical action of Christians in gathering at special times and places for worship? Does the same freedom characterize the worship of Christians in the world where the legal system still pertains? With their belief in Jesus as the expected Messiah, Christians undoubtedly perceived that something new had erupted in history that required a reassessment of the very grounds of worship. Worship now took place in the name of Jesus and in the freedom of his spirit. How were these assemblies for worship in the name of Jesus to be understood, and what form were they to take? Could Christian worship continue within the religious categories of ritual and cult, or did its freedom in the spirit make it fundamentally different and, therefore, discontinuous with any cult, however much it might resemble the cult in some aspects?

Liturgical studies have generally noted the many continuities between the emerging Christian cult and both Jewish and pagan cults. Continuity between Jewish and Christian worship, it is acknowledged, gave to Christian worship much of both its shape and content. Even that most Christian of prayers, the Lord's Prayer, can be accounted for almost entirely within the realm of Hebrew religious expression. And well known are the Jewish

36

antecedents of the Eucharist: in the synagogue service of scripture reading and prayer and in the meal of the Upper Room, whether this is regarded as a *Chaburah*, the common religious meal celebrated among Jewish friends, or as a special Passover meal. Both Jewish and pagan antecedents can also be found for the initiation rite of Baptism and for the liturgy of time that provides the framework within which the nonsacramental services of daily prayer as well as sacramental services are celebrated.

How these continuities with Jewish worship are to be assessed has been a matter of much debate among scholars. Some have seen the authenticity of Christian worship in the continuity between Christian and Jewish worship, while denying any connection with pagan cults. Others have sought an early authentic expression of worship in scripture that was discontinuous with cultic worship, but gradually assumed features of the cults, both pagan and Jewish, as the initial inspiration declined. Where the continuity with the cults has been regarded as intrinsic to Christian worship, as in the Catholic tradition, the question of freedom has usually not been considered vital. However, freedom in worship, as expressed in most Protestant denominations, has often been asserted in opposition to the cults.

Our question, in keeping with the apocalyptic vision of worship, is whether Christian liturgy is a ritual cult of freedom. This manner of posing the question allows for both continuity and discontinuity with cultic practices, whether Jewish or pagan.

Whereas most treatments of the history of liturgy have dealt with the development of the structure and outer forms of the liturgy, our concern with freedom will lead us to seek to uncover the attitudes that accompany and inform liturgical practice. The evidence for these attitudes can be found not only in the liturgy itself, but also in the whole range of the life of faith. Before proceeding to the question of freedom in worship I shall begin with the broader question of how the freedom of the gospel is to be understood in the whole life of the Christian. The most fully developed treatment of the Christian understanding of law and freedom in the New Testament is found in the writings of Paul, to which I now turn.

Paul depicts Christian freedom in the world, where the law still governs, as an inner detachment from the world. "I know how to be abased, and I know how to abound; in any and all circumstances I have learned the secret of facing plenty and hunger, abundance and want [Phil. 4:12]." The inner detachment depicted in this passage would appear to parallel what is to be found in other religions. It bears a remarkable resemblance, for example, to the "equal-mindedness" that characterizes the enlightened person in *The Bhagavadgita*.

When one has conquered one's self (lower) and has attained to the calm of self-mastery, his Supreme Self abides ever concentrate, he is at peace in cold and heat, in pleasure and pain, in honour and dishonour.[1]

This form of detachment is achieved only after a long process of self-discipline called yoga. The response to the passivity of life, which is identified as attachment and bodily desire, is to assume perfect control of one's self by concentrating the mind. But herein lies the difference from Paul's understanding of freedom. Christian freedom, according to Paul, does not come as the end result of a long process of religious discipline. Worship in Christianity does not serve this function. For faith is an attribute, not only of the wise or powerful or those of noble birth (1 Corinthians 1:26), but of the poor and weak. Jesus indeed held up little children as supreme examples of faith.[2] Attainment of the freedom of faith is not by self-discipline, but by invitation. Disciples are those who answer Jesus' call, "Follow me."

Paul attributes his mastery in life not to his own inner strength or self-mastery, but to the grace of Christ. He continues to say, following the passage previously quoted, "I can do all things in him who strengthens me [Phil. 4:13]." Nor is this strength to be understood as merely adding to Paul's own limited strength. It is paradoxically revealed in his weakness, which corresponds with the weakness of Christ on the cross. When Paul prays to God to be delivered from an infirmity, his prayer is not answered as he expects. For he hears God say to him: "My grace is sufficient for you, for my power is made perfect in weakness." To this Paul responds:

I will all the more gladly boast of my weaknesses, that the power of Christ may rest upon me. For the sake of Christ, then, I am content with weaknesses, insults, hardships, persecutions, and calamities; for when I am weak, then I am strong. (2 Cor. 12:9–10)

With this attitude of inner detachment Paul is free to enter fully into the world. And so he urges his readers to participate in the full range of experiences of ordinary life: "Rejoice with those who rejoice, weep with those who weep [Rom. 12:15]." This attitude of the faithful can be contrasted with the prevailing outlook that seeks happiness and fulfillment in life (mastery) by avoiding all the circumstances that could cause pain or sorrow (passivity), while pursuing pleasure wherever it may be found.

Paul describes the freedom of faith, therefore, as a dialectic of involvement and inner detachment:

I mean, brethren, the appointed time has grown very short; from now on, let those who have wives live as though they had none, and those who mourn as though they were not mourning, and those who rejoice as though they were not rejoicing, and those who buy as though they had no goods, and those who deal with the world as though they had no dealings with it. For the form of this world is passing away. (1 Cor. 7:29–31)

In this paradoxical "as though not" Paul is expressing a peculiar disjunction and continuity between reality as the Christian experiences it in faith, and reality as ordinarily experienced. The Christian participates fully in ordinary experience but is not bound to make the characteristic response that the circumstances would appear to call for. The faithful are free to make an uncharacteristic response because they take their cue from a different Ruler than the ruling powers in nature and history. This freedom of outlook is profoundly eschatological because it is grounded in an understanding that the world, where these powers still rule, is rapidly passing away. The Christian is already living according to the standards of the New Age that is to come, not apart from this current age, but within this age, "as though not." Vis-à-vis the existing ruling powers the stance of the Christian, then, is a subversive one.

This eschatological outlook, which overturns the world, can be traced to the parables of the kingdom in Jesus' preaching. According to John D. Crossan, in contrast to the apocalyptic eschatology that looked to the end of this world, Jesus spoke out of a prophetic eschatology that overturns all worlds. "Be it the world of demonic possession, of enriched security, or, of Pharisaic righteousness, the kingdom is that which in shaking man's world at its foundations establishes the dominion of God over and against all such worlds."³ Of the subversive nature of the advent of the kingdom Crossan writes:

The kingdom's advent is that which undermines world so that we can experience God as distinct from world, and the action and life which the kingdom demands is built upon this insecurity. Our ethical principles and our moral systems are absolutely necessary and so also is their inevitable shattering as part and parcel of the shattering of world. We walk a knife-edge between absolutism on the one hand and indifference on the other.⁴

The language of Jesus' parables is, according to Crossan, metaphorical. It belongs to the ordinary sphere of daily life and yet points beyond it to the kingdom that is breaking in. And so Jesus tells of a sower who goes forth to sow, a woman who discovers a lost coin, a marriage feast to which a number are invited—stories of ordinary events. But they become the vehicle for the extraordinary—not the extraordinary as religiously understood in terms of the supernatural, the sacral, or the occult, but the extraordinary paradoxically perceived in the ordinary. They are stories of extraordinary harvests in unpromising circumstances, of the joy attendant on finding a lost coin, of a surprising new guest list for the wedding when the original guests decline the invitation. How or whether worship is an expression of an eschatological freedom that Paul expresses as a paradoxical "as though not" and Crossan, as "the knife-edge between absolutism . . . and indifference" is the question to which we now turn.

For a more direct treatment of the question of freedom as it pertains to worship in the New Testament I shall primarily refer to Ferdinand Hahn's valuable study *The Worship of the Early Church*. As a biblical scholar, Hahn adduces his evidence for early Christian worship from the full range of biblical witness, not only from references to worship practices. This breadth of study will help in discovering the attitudes that accompany the worship and, to a great extent, give it its distinctive character. Using the tradition-history method, Hahn seeks to avoid making generalizations about worship that do not take into account the various communities and periods represented in the New Testament. He is concerned above all to avoid reading later liturgical developments into early material, as has often been done by liturgical historians, seeking the scriptural foundations for such ecclesiastical institutions as Baptism, Eucharist, and Ministry.

Hahn depicts early Christian worship as an exercise of freedom arising out of "the newness of God's eschatological acts" in Jesus Christ. "What is eschatologically new imposes itself in concrete form taking hold of what is old and reshaping it."[5] What emerges, he maintains, is not simply an adaptation of the worship of Judaism—regardless of how many individual features of this worship reappear in Christian worship—but something entirely novel. The novelty in Christian worship arises out of a rejection of "Jewish observance of the law and its concomitant ritualization of life"[6] in the temple cult. In Christian worship the separation of the sacred and secular that is fundamental to the whole of ancient thought, including the temple cult, no longer pertains.

For the Christian community worship does not take place in a separate realm but in the midst of the existing world; it therefore includes service by the faithful in everyday life. Christian worship is no longer cultic in nature.[7]

Hahn finds this new attitude toward worship expressed in a variety of ways in the different New Testament communities. It is seen in the practice of all the communities of worshiping *kat 'oikon* (in a house). Worship no longer takes place "within well defined and sanctified precincts."[8] In the Hellenistic Jewish community Stephen is persecuted for his attack on the Jerusalem temple cult (Acts 6:13–14). But cultic ideas are not simply discarded by the Christian. There is rather a "spiritualization" of Jewish cultic ideas that allows "a certain transference of cultic language to noncultic phenomena."[9] Cultic terminology is now applied Christologically and ecclesiologically. The earthly temple, for example, becomes an eschatological temple that refers to Christ (John 2:19) and to the Easter community (Mark 14:58). The language of sacrifice is also given a different referent. The idea of the Passover lamb is made to refer to the sacrifice of Christ (1 Corinthians 5:7); and the idea of a "living sacrifice" *(thysia)* as a "spiritual worship" *(logike latreia)* (Romans 12:1) refers to the Christian's life in the world. This transference plays a significant role in appropriating the whole of life into the sphere of worship instead of confining worship to a sacral area only.

Worship in the early gentile communities exhibits a strong reliance on the work of the Spirit, which is understood as an eschatological gift. The free expression of the Spirit accounts for the "astounding variety" in the worship of the Corinthian church[10] (1 Corinthians 14). The role of women prophesying in worship (1 Corinthians 11:2–16) may show the influence of the prophecy in Joel, "Your sons and your daughters shall prophesy [2:28]," contrary to the regulations excluding women from an active role that governed the synagogue. Christian worship also has a strong communal aspect as opposed to the individual piety of the cults. In his statement on the Lord's Supper in 1 Corinthians 10:16 Paul uses the word *koinonia*—*koinonia* of the blood in the cup and *koinonia* of the body of Christ in the bread that we break. This word, which is translated as "communion," is to be understood not simply as comradeship among the communicants, but, in a much stronger corporate sense, as "partaking of" or "sharing" the body and blood of Christ.[11] Christians do not merely come to receive the elements of communion. In eating and drinking together they are united with one another in Christ. The Lord's Supper is a communal action that calls for an active participation on the part of the communicant.

Paul makes clear that worship extends beyond the immediate assembly for worship into acts of service in the world (Romans 12). Where an apparently overly sacramentalized celebration of the Lord's Supper leads to an abuse of worship in Corinth, the problem can be rectified, according to Paul, only by a changed ethical relationship in the community (1 Corinthians 11:17ff.). All these shifts in attitude toward worship are susceptible to reverting back to earlier ones, thus losing the original novelty and freedom of worship. And so the issue around circumcision prompts Paul to admonish the Galatians: "For freedom Christ has set us free; stand fast therefore, and do not submit again to a yoke of slavery [Gal. 5:1]."

There can be no mistaking that in the minds of the early Christians their new approach to worship was a direct outcome of God's saving action as revealed in the cross and resurrection of Jesus Christ and continued in the power of the Holy Spirit. But they were guided no less by attitudes toward worship exhibited by Jesus throughout his ministry. His attitude can be discerned in a number of ways. It is evident in his willingness to heal on the sabbath or to allow his disciples to pluck ears of grain, thus breaking the sabbath law. He also disregards the regulations that govern cleanness and uncleanness by eating and drinking with tax collectors and sinners, and in his saying that there is nothing outside a person that, by going into him or her, can defile; but the things that come out of a person are what defile (Mark 7:15). Jesus attacks prayer viewed as "a pious work" and affirms it as an "expression of confidence" growing out of an intimate relationship with God,[12] whom he addresses as *Abba*. On the basis of such a relationship the following affirmation about prayer can be understood: "Whatever you ask in prayer, believe that you have received it, and it will be yours [Mark 11:24]."

In Jesus' fellowship meals, as Hahn notes, the cultic split between the sacred and the profane is broken down. He writes:

Jesus' repasts thus reveal quite concretely the significance of his conduct with respect to the liturgical ordinances of Judaism; here all ritual precepts are set aside by virtue of sovereign authority, all walls separating the sacred from the profane are torn down. These acts of table fellowship take place in the midst of daily life, and no one remains excluded from the act of worship.[13]

Jesus' attitude toward the temple cult is more difficult to discern. We know that he made a practice of attending the synagogue and on more than one occasion took an active part in its service (Luke 4:16–30). Jesus also went to Jerusalem at the time of the Passover as the custom was. There is no evidence, however, for his participation in the sacrificial cult of the temple, although his driving of the money changers out of the temple is reported in all four Gospels. It is disputed, however, whether this action was a "cleansing of the temple" for the sake of a truer sacrifice, or an action that made the cult impossible by removing its material basis. Even the stricture in Matthew 5:23–24 that calls for the worshiper to be reconciled with a brother or sister before offering a gift is not unequivocally advocating a more proper exercise of the sacrificial cult. On the contrary, this interruption of a cultic act indicates that something "matters more" than the performance of the ritual.[14]

It is in Jesus' claim to be able to forgive sins, according to Hahn, that the "propitiatory system of the temple" is most clearly abrogated. The accusation of blasphemy brought against Jesus in Mark 2:5ff. is not without reason.[15] The post-Easter community rightly says of Jesus, "What is here is greater than the temple" (Matthew 12:6).

The whole of Jesus' life and ministry presented an undeniable challenge to the contemporary Jewish worship practice as exemplified in the temple cult, with its underlying dualism of the sacred and the profane, its ritual separation from daily life, and its observance of law rather than freedom. From our earlier observations about Hebrew worship we may see in Jesus' attitude to the cult a prophetic protest against abuses of the cult in the manner of earlier prophets. It is not accurate to the Hebrew understanding simply to oppose Torah to freedom, or cult to doing justice. New Testament worship is taking place in the context of contemporary Jewish practice that has become highly legalistic. It is possible, therefore, to understand Jesus' action as a prophetic protest. This conclusion does not, in itself, however, take fully into account the radical implications that the early Christians attributed to Jesus as the Messiah representing God's eschatological saving action. That the eschatological outlook of awaiting the Messiah had made its mark already on Hebrew worship prevents any claim for an absolute breach between Jewish and Christian worship. The coming of the Messiah, however, with the accompanying eschatological sign of the Spirit's presence is going to bring a new reality into worship that will alter all previous expectations. Jesus' saying about not putting new wine into old wine skins is inevitably going to be applied to worship. But how is this worship in the Spirit to be understood, and what form will it take?

The most general picture that emerged included what Alexander Schmemann has called a "liturgical dualism"[16] of worship in the synagogue and temple, and "breaking bread together" at home after the manner of the meal in the Upper Room. Hahn points out that although a form of unified worship constituting a service of word and meal fellowship crystallized during the second century, this cannot "be considered the only possible and necessary outcome."[17] As significant as this was for the worship of the Christian

44

church over many centuries, it is Hahn's judgment that "the price paid was the loss of the original wealth and of liturgical vitality."[18] Hahn leaves open the question of how the movement from the relatively unstructured community to the later more ordered system of the early Catholic Church is to be judged.[19] He does, however, show an appreciation for a free expression of worship where the working of the Spirit is not quenched. He acknowledges that spirit and order are not irreconcilable, but that order and law are consistent with freedom only if they are not codified.[20] Whether cultic ritual is consistent with freedom of worship appears, however, to be precluded by Hahn's claim that Jesus renounced "temple worship and all cultic and ritual practices."[21]

Hahn appears to confine the notions of cult and ritual to practices designed to effect salvation in a sacral sphere apart from ordinary life. This kind of worship, he maintains, Jesus clearly rejected. But Hahn does acknowledge a "salvific action in worship"[22] based on an understanding of worship as primarily God's service to human beings, to which our human service in "obedience, prayer and confession of faith is always a response."[23] This affirmation raises the question whether cult and ritual may appropriately continue in Christian worship with a radically transformed religious motive behind them. Hahn's unequivocal rejection of ritual and cult would appear to preclude such a possibility. But his account of early attitudes toward worship may, nevertheless, offer some clues for a transformed practice of ritual and cult now experienced as a celebration of freedom.

A first clue can be found in Jesus' rejection of prayer as a pious work while encouraging a confident attitude in prayer. The early Christians assumed this attitude in their own worship and prayer in "the name of" or "through Jesus Christ." Perhaps this confidence is nowhere more clearly stated than by the writer of the letter to the Hebrews, who uses the language of the sacrificial cult of the temple:

Therefore, brethren, since we have confidence to enter the sanctuary by the blood of Jesus, by the new and living way which he opened for us through the curtain, that is, through his flesh, and since we have a great priest over the house of God, let us draw near with a true heart in full assurance of faith, with our hearts sprinkled clean from an evil conscience and our bodies washed with pure water. Let us hold fast the confession of our hope without wavering, for he who promised is faithful; and let us consider how to stir up one another to love and good works, not neglecting to meet together, as is the habit of some, but encouraging one another, and all the more as you see the Day drawing near. (Heb. 10:19–25)

Here is an entirely different perception of the relationship between humanity and God than the usual religious one that seeks to influence and placate God. And yet prayer itself does not cease. Indeed it is made even more central to the life of faith than it ever was in the religious realm, to the point where Paul can speak of praying "without ceasing" (1 Thessalonians 5:17). Clearly this Christian prayer is no longer a partial aspect of life, but has become coextensive with the whole life of faith—a communion with a God who is not to be met with in a separate sacral sphere, but in the midst of life. Prayer then becomes an expression for the openness and vulnerability toward the world that we saw in Paul's account of Christian freedom.

And yet there are times for prayer in the life of the Christian. These times do not serve the religious purpose of bringing about communion with God. The Christian is already confident of that. They are, rather, as a liturgy of time, ways of marking time, by bringing every moment of time into the eschatological time of God's new age that is entering into history through Jesus Christ. And this time of worship and prayer is not marked by fear or a posture of prostration before a superior being, but by an attitude of mutual communion in which dignity, joy and sorrow, hope and caring for one another can be expressed.

Schmemann has spoken of the tone of this worship as, on the one hand, an "inner solemnity" in which "the fullness of religious meaning [can be] invested in an action, no matter how simple it may be."[24]

External solemnity, on the other hand, consists in the sacralization of sacred ceremonies and actions, in emphasizing that they are not "simple," in building around them an atmosphere of sacred and religious fear which cannot fail to influence the way they are received and experienced by the participants in the cult.[25]

In speaking of the "inner solemnity" of the Christian liturgy,

Schmemann is no doubt thinking of something like the paradoxical "as though not" of faith as expressed in worship, similar to the seriousness with which children play their games of make-believe. This childlike attitude of play, which psychologists tell us is the child's way of appropriating her or his world,[26] is right for worship as an "eschatological game."[27] And of course for this action the rituals of the cult are appropriate but now invested with an entirely new meaning.

For this change of meaning in the language and actions of the cult that makes them acceptable to Christian worship we find another clue in what Hahn calls the "transferred use of cultic terminology in the New Testament."[28] By this he means that the cultic ideas used to characterize the temple worship and its sacrificial cult are used instead "to describe the Christ-event or the conduct of Christians in the world."[29] Hahn rightly sees in this "transference of cultic language to noncultic phenomena"[30] an opening of worship to the world by removing worship from its separate sphere. "There is," he says, "no longer any distinction in principle between assembly for worship and the service of Christians in the world."[31]

But how did the transference of cultic language do this? Hahn answers this question by speaking of a "spiritualization" of cultic ideas. Hahn is using the term to refer to a shift from the objective reality of the cult and its rituals, to the spiritual and moral conduct of the Christian in the world. But the shift is more than from physical and objective categories to spiritual and personal ones, as the term spiritualization usually implies. There are objective and physical aspects associated with both the cult and the behavior of Christians in the world. Harold W. Turner has addressed this question with reference to Jesus' use of language pertaining to the temple to speak of himself.

This meant more than the spiritualization of worship that was a common enough quest in the Graeco-Roman world; it did more than replace the material temple by the temple of the soul or spirit of man and so make the meeting place with the divine founders, subjective and spiritual. The physical place of meeting erected "with hands" was to be replaced by something equally objective but "not made with hands," by a personal meeting place to be found where both body and spirit united in the totality of his own person. He was the new temple, the positive replacement for all temples and cults on the Jerusalem pattern. His own body, whether interpreted individually or also corporately as the church, was the visible and historical reality that had become "the medium for transcending the material and revealing spiritual qualities through the material."[32]

Turner prefers the word personalization[33] to "spiritualization" for this phenomenon. It is a personalization that takes on "visible and historical" form in the person of Jesus and in the corporate reality of the community that follows Jesus or lives "in Christ."

The community, one may go on to affirm, contrary to Hahn's notion of spiritualization, gives expression to the visible and historical reality of Christ in both its liturgy and in its life in the world. It does this not in any impersonal way, as the *ex opera operato* function of a cult enacted in a separate sacral sphere, but in the personal form of a community gathered in the midst of the world for prayer and praise, and being sent forth to continue its worship through concrete actions of Christian love in the world. For both the actions of the liturgy and the ethical actions in the world, words, symbols, and gestures are necessary to give them form and expression. Neither the ethical actions nor the symbolic actions of the liturgy— or what Northrop Frye has called the "language of concern" and the "language of metaphor"—that together constitute the *kerygma* or proclamation in the Bible,[34] can occur authentically in isolation from each other. Of the relationship between liturgy and life, Monika Hellwig has said that "the response in symbolic ritual is supposed to evoke an understanding of what the response in the whole of life must be."[35] The Christ-event, which constitutes the eschatological dawning of God's rule in the world, embraces both. For a way of accurately describing the event that embraces both the reality of our ordinary existence, expressed in worship and daily life, and the coming eschatological reality, including both the tension and the continuity between the two, I propose that we look to the concept of metaphor. "Metaphor" is a notoriously slippery and hard-to-define term in modern language study. For our purposes I shall begin by referring to the capacity of metaphor to connect and hold together in tension two dissimilar realities without losing either.

There is a primitive understanding of metaphor that attributes to words and symbols the power to *effect* that which they signify. "This is that." This understanding is at the root of all magic-sacrificial ritual. In placing the efficacy not in the ritual, but in God's saving action in the world, Jesus repudiated this original sense of metaphor. But there is another sense of metaphor that, while rejecting any direct powers in the word or thing in itself, does attribute to them the power to point beyond themselves and so to bring to light what is hidden and to make that which is absent present.[36] Metaphor, in this sense, has the ability to hold both "is" and "is not" together without lessening the contradiction between the two. Metaphors say both "this is that" and "this is not that,"[37] expressing a relationship of identity and nonidentity. Worship, viewed as metaphor, holds together the *now* and *not yet* of the future that is promised by God. This future that is "not yet" in our experience of daily life can be anticipated and celebrated in the present in the church's rituals.

The function of metaphors, as John D. Crossan has noted in his discussion of parables, is to enable participation.[38] We are talking of what, in the general religious view, is considered to be two separate realities—the reality of the world and the reality of the divine. Metaphors, with their "tensive discontinuous and surprising nature,"[39] bring together both realities in a paradoxical identity. Metaphors enable participation in both realities at once. As such, the rituals, understood like the parables, as metaphors, can be vehicles of transcendence, experienced not in a separate sacred sphere, but as the extraordinary in the ordinary.

Without the metaphors as expressed and embodied in the rituals of worship, the Christian community is always in danger of losing the extraordinary reality that now encompasses the whole of its life. The ritual is not a means of salvation, understood as effecting God's saving action in the world apart from daily life. The ritual is, rather, a metaphor of salvation in the sense of proclaiming to, or bringing before, the community of faith the saving action of God that is occurring throughout the lives of the faithful, and indeed beyond their lives, in the whole world. By such means the faithful are enabled to participate in what God is doing in the world. That the ritual as metaphor evokes another world besides the current one—God's reign that is the future of this world—gives to worship a subversive effect in relation to the ruling powers of this world. I shall give further consideration to this power of metaphor in chapter 7. At this point I can say of the ritual of Christian worship, as I see it in the New Testament, that it is both a celebration of freedom as an act of praise and a means of empowering people for living in the freedom of faith in the world. This freedom entails making, what I referred to earlier in my examination of Paul's writings, an "uncharacteristic response."

Because of a metaphorical shift the early Christians were able to reappropriate the language of ritual and cult not only for their theology, which Hahn acknowledges,[40] but for the enactment of their faith in worship. There is a risk in such a move that the new intention will get lost and that the worshiping community will lapse back into idolatry and legalism. The history of the church is a witness to both the danger and the promise of ritual worship. The melancholy fact we have now to acknowledge is that through much of its history, the worship of the church has been celebrated, not as a sign of freedom, but as an exercise of the church's authority, and it has been left to means other than worship to seek and express human freedom. In the history of Western civilization, philosophy rather than worship became the champion of the cause of freedom over against the authority of the church.

PART TWO

Modern Obstacles and New Possibilities

4

Freedom and Authority in Conflict

The celebration of freedom in early Christian worship within a very short time began to give way to the current legalities of culture and religion. One of the earliest symptoms of a shift was the denial to women of the right to speak in the worship assembly.[1] At the same time a move was taking place from charismatic to an official leadership. Although this was not necessarily a denial of freedom, it became so, as the clergy gradually became a separate order with their own reason for being, apart from their service to the community.[2] By the fourth century there were signs that the attitude of confidence in worship was being replaced by a desire to influence and placate God in the manner of the sacrificial cults. The elements of bread and wine in the Eucharist had become objects of religious fear to be handled only by priests who were consecrated for this holy task. From being a holy people participating in a communal action of worship, worshipers were being transformed into passive recipients of the ministrations of a holy priesthood. Passivity in worship could hardly be symbolized more clearly than by the practice of receiving the bread directly on the tongue in order that it not be touched by unholy hands.[3]

The emerging authority of the church in the Roman Empire was given expression in what Schmemann has called the "external solemnity" of the cult.[4] The imperial court ceremonies began to appear in Christian worship: in the design of buildings, now once again regarded as sacred precincts, elaborate vestments, processions of clergy, and so on. The people were being relegated to the status of onlookers as worship became increasingly clericalized. This process became complete when the people's part in present-

53

ing the bread and wine at the altar table was dispensed with, about the eleventh century,[5] in favor of an altar prepared by the clergy.

The authority of the church was given a metaphysical base with the appropriation of the Greek cosmological system. It posited a dualism of the natural and supernatural and an arrangement of all things in heaven and on earth in a hierarchy or chain of being from the lowest inanimate object to the highest spiritual reality. The ascending orders of angels in heaven were mirrored in the hierarchy of clergy in the church. Worship was a reflection or focusing of a sacramental universe in which all things participated in the reality of the divine by an analogy of being *(analogia entis)*.

The church's sacraments were vehicles of the divine presence to be offered or withheld according to the will of the ecclesiastical authorities. By such means the church was able to exercise authority even over princes, who gave in to the threat of excommunication when confronted with the possible loss of the grace on which their souls depended for eternal life.

Within the comprehensive legal system of the official cult the freedom of the gospel was greatly diminished, only to emerge in a variety of other ways, including the devotional life of the mystics, the prayer life in some monasteries and convents, the beneficent actions of individual Christians on behalf of the poor and needy, and the creative work of artists, philosophers, and theologians. It is to the study of philosophy that we have to look for a development that was eventually to challenge decisively the authority of the church in the interests of human freedom. This story has to be told in order to understand the place worship can have in modern life as a liturgy of praise and empowerment after the secular emancipation from the sacral authority has taken place.

Freedom emerged in philosophy in opposition to the ecclesiastical authority of scripture, dogma, and sacrament as a growing awareness of the autonomous power of human reason. Religion and worship were perceived to be rooted in the passivity of life and were, therefore, a hindrance to the attainment of mastery. The preoccupation of philosophy with the latter led to an eventual divergence of philosophy from worship, although for much of church history, philosophy existed in the service of worship, sharing with worship the same metaphysical outlook.

Already in Greek philosophy, which provided the conceptual language for the Christian philosophy of the Middle Ages, there can be seen a growing breach between philosophical thought and popular religion. The notion of God, it is true, occupied a key place in Greek systems of thought, as in Plato's idea of "The Form of the Good" and Aristotle's "Unmoved Mover." But God was considered to be more akin to the human power of thought and moral will than to instincts such as wonder and gratitude that give rise to worship.

Christian metaphysics shared the Greek confidence in the power of the mind and its speculation to comprehend the idea of God. But there was also the recognition that faith has priority over reason. Reason is at the service of religion, as "faith seeking understanding" (*fides quaerens intellectum*), to use a phrase made famous by Anselm. Anselm's ontological argument for the existence of God, which begins from the idea of a Perfect Being and then posits the existence of that Being as necessary to its perfection, is an act of reasoning that begins and ends in worship. Anselm concludes an extremely intricate line of reasoning as follows:

No one, indeed, understanding what God is can think that God does not exist. . . . For God is that-than-which-nothing-greater-can-be-thought. Whoever really understands this understands clearly that this same being so exists that not even in thought can it not exist. Thus whoever understands that God exists in such a way cannot think of Him as not existing.

I give thanks, good Lord, I give thanks to You, since what I believed before through Your free gift I now so understand through Your illumination, that if I did not want to *believe* that You existed, I should nevertheless be unable not to *understand* it.[6]

Here is a process of reasoning within which the attributes of worship—wonder and gratitude—are far from being alien.

The pattern of passivity and mastery, which, as observed, shapes the religious consciousness, appears in philosophy as the problem of the contingency of created being. Thomas Aquinas, the great medieval theologian, in his third proof for the existence of God, argued from contingent to necessary being, starting from the fact that some beings come into existence and then perish. These beings are contingent and not necessary, for if they were necessary they would always have existed, neither coming into being nor passing away. Aquinas, then, argued for the existence of a necessary being without whom contingent beings would not have come into being and indeed nothing would exist. Frederick Copleston has maintained that this third proof from contingency is the fundamental proof for the existence of God in Aquinas' philosophy, underlying all his proofs.

In the first proof the argument from contingency is applied to the special fact of motion or change, in the second proof to the order of causality or causal production, in the fourth proof to finality, to the operation of inorganic objects in the attainment of cosmic order.[7]

In this brief sample of metaphysical speculation can be seen the same presupposition of an ordered universe and awareness of the givenness of life as underlie Christian worship. But it is also possible to see how a living God who dwells in mystery, but continually reaches out in loving care to human beings, is replaced by one who is a mere object of rational speculation. This development occurred in Western philosophy in the form of deism, the philosophical view that God is necessary to account for the existence of all things but has no continuing relationship with creation. The analogy of the Divine Clockmaker adequately expressed the mechanistic nature of the deistic universe. Mystery and, of course, worship were inconsistent with the God of the deists. Thomas Aquinas perhaps sensed the dangers in philosophical speculation when, as the story goes, he came, near the end of his life, to characterize all his philosophical labors as so much "straw." Future generations do not agree with this humble assessment of the "angelic doctor's" philosophical endeavors.

The trend in philosophy away from worship was already well on its way by the time of the Protestant Reformation, this being a factor, no doubt, in the Reformers' reaction against the philosophical tradition in theology. For Luther the primary question in theology was not, as in philosophy, "Does God exist?" or "What is God in his own nature?" but rather, "Is God for or against me?" His concern about a gracious God led him to focus his theology on what God has done and is doing for the salvation of God's creation. Luther found the certainty of salvation in his knowledge of what God has done in Christ and, in particular, the cross of Christ. This emphasis led him to give priority to the word of scripture *(sola scriptura)*, which attests to Christ's saving work. Worship became for Luther the occasion for preaching and responding to the "living Word of God" *(Viva vox Dei)* in word and sacrament.

In the theology of both Luther and Calvin a strong awareness of the givenness of life is expressed, not in philosophical argument, but in faith's affirmation of the power of God, who every moment upholds creation in being. Luther commented on the first article of the Apostles' Creed, which deals with God's creative activity.

This is the supreme article of faith of which we speak: I believe in God the Father almighty, maker of heaven and earth. And whoever honestly believes this is already helped and is once again brought back to the place whence Adam fell. But few are they who go so far as to believe fully that he is the God who makes and creates all things. For such a man must be dead to everything, to good and bad, to death and life, to hell and heaven, and must confess in his heart that he is able to do nothing by his own power.[8]

Here Luther is setting faith's affirmation of God as Creator over the philosophical view by asserting the utter passivity of the human creature before "the God who makes and creates all things."

Calvin, too, objected to the limited philosophical understanding of God as Creator by affirming in its place God's continuing and providential rule over creation. He wrote:

Without proceeding to His Providence, we cannot understand the full force of what is meant by God being the Creator, how much soever we may seem to comprehend it with our mind, and confess it with our tongue. The carnal mind, when once it has perceived the power of God in creation, stops there, and at the farthest, thinks and ponders on nothing else than the wisdom, power and goodness displayed by the Author of such a work . . . , or on some general agency on which the power of emotion depends, exercised in preserving and governing it. In short it imagines that all things are sufficiently sustained by the energy divinely infused into them at first. But faith penetrates deeper. After learning that there is a Creator, it must forthwith infer that he is also a Governor and Preserver, and that, not by producing a kind of general motion in the making of the globe as well as in each of its parts, but by a special Providence sustaining and cherishing, superintending, all the things which he has made, to the very minutest, even to a sparrow.[9]

With their references to "believing *fully* . . . in the God who makes and creates all things" and "understanding *the full force* of what is meant by God being the Creator," both Luther and Calvin wanted to go beyond mere comprehension of a truth of reason to lively awareness of the believer's dependence on God that can issue in worship. But this line of reasoning tended to reinforce the connection between worship and passivity, thereby confirming the emerging split between philosophical reasoning, with its preoccupation with mastery and freedom, and a worship rooted and grounded in passivity. Their criticism of the sacrificial and magical tendencies of medieval worship in the interests of the freedom of the gospel, it is true, might have led to a recovery of the original motivation in Christian worship. But it led them, at the same time, to diminish the symbolic content of worship, with an attendant loss of the participation of the people. If worshipers hitherto had been passive onlookers, they now became passive listeners, as the preached Word took the place of the priestly mass. Cultic expression of worship also was called in question by the Reformers' recovery, through their biblical study, of worship as being expressed in the whole of life. This secularizing of worship was taken to the extreme, in parts of the Radical Reformation and later Protestant liberalism, of seeking to abolish ritual acts of worship altogether.

The legacy of the Reformation with regard to the celebration of freedom in worship was, it appears, a mixed one. It is beyond question that Luther had a profound sense of the freedom of the gospel, as he found it expressed in the writings of Paul. But he retained the strong medieval sense of dependence on God experienced in human passivity. His debate with Erasmus over the question of the freedom of the will reveals where Luther stood in relation to the growing awareness of human powers in Renaissance humanism. Whereas Erasmus' book was entitled *The Freedom of the Will*, Luther's was *The Bondage of the Will*. What Luther had to say about the freedom of the Christian being rooted in the grace of God was to go unheard by the philosophy of the day. For the humanists, talk of the grace of God ran counter to their understanding of human autonomy. Freedom, it appeared to them, could only be affirmed in opposition to the authority of the scriptures, the teaching and worship of the church. Their efforts came to fulfillment in the Enlightenment of the eighteenth century, when a complete breach occurred between the unfettered use of the mind and the traditional ecclesiastical authority. Enlightenment philosophy rejected both the metaphysics and the worship of the church.

Immanuel Kant's definition of *Aufklärung* (enlightenment) reveals the new sense of human autonomy as opposed to religious or metaphysical control over the mind. To the question: "What is enlightenment?" he replied:

The enlightenment represents man's emergence from a self-inflicted state of minority. A minor is one who is incapable of making use of his understanding without guidance from someone else. This minority is self-inflicted whenever its cause lies not in the lack of understanding, but in lack of the determination and courage to make use of it without the guidance of another. *Sapere Audi!* Have the courage to make use of your own understanding, is therefore the watchword of the Enlightenment. [10]

Kant had no intention of opposing religion altogether. Rather, he stated as the objective of his *Critique of Pure Reason* to "deny knowledge in order to make room for faith."[11] His insistence, with the empirical philosophers of the day, that "objective knowledge does not reach beyond the data of objective experience,"[12] however, called in question the supernatural basis of revealed religion and metaphysics, including the traditional proofs for the existence of God. As an idealist, moreover, Kant posited an active rather than a passive mind, thus giving priority to the freedom of the human subject over the objective world. This, we shall see in his followers, became a basis for asserting the absolute autonomy of human being.

Whereas Kant rejected revealed religion with its ceremonies of worship, he did affirm a natural religion rooted in the moral law. The God who was lost to reason now became a postulate of the moral will. Kant was capable of regarding the moral law, seen in the light of reason, with the awe and wonder usually reserved for the mysterious God of revealed religion.

Duty! Thou sublime and mighty name that dost embrace nothing charming or insinuating, but requirest submission, and yet seekest not to move the will by threatening aught that would arouse natural aversion or terror, but merely holdest forth a law which of itself finds entrance into the mind . . . a law before which all inclinations are dumb, even though they secretly counterwork it; what origin is there worthy of thee?[13]

In this moral religion there is only one true service of God that consists "not in dogmas and rites but in the heart's disposition to fulfil all human duties as divine commands."[14] Besides this higher spirituality Kant does allow some validity to religious ceremonies. He acknowledges that communion at the Lord's Table may "contain within itself something great, expanding the narrow, selfish and unsociable cast of mind among men especially in matters of religion."[15] But "to incorporate among the articles of faith the proposition that this ceremony, which is after all but a churchly act, is, in addition, a means of grace—this is a religious illusion which can do naught but work counter to the spirit of religion."[16]

The firmness of Kant's convictions in rejecting revealed religion with its worship practices is perhaps exemplified by the story that is told of him on the occasion of an academic procession to a service of worship in the university church in Konigsberg, where he was a professor. Kant dutifully accompanied the procession on its way until it came to the door of the church, where Kant was seen to veer away as the others entered for worship.

Kant's critique of metaphysics and revealed religion in the name of the autonomous power of reason and the will did not bring about a total rejection of religion. But he did unseat religion from its place at the pinnacle of human life by relegating it to the realm of morality, which indeed Kant took to be a higher spirituality than that which could be attained by religious ritual and dogma. It was, however, but a small step for some of his idealist followers to assert the autonomy of human being in such a way as to deny religion altogether.

This happened in the great atheistic controversy at the beginning of the nineteenth century, initiated by Johann Gottlieb Fichte and Friedrich Wilhelm Joseph von Schelling. The issue was over the self-sufficiency of humanity over against the Christian view that human beings derive their being from God. Fichte asserted the doctrine of human selfhood as self-constituting in an essay that started the controversy:

Nothing other than the self may be assumed as the ground in terms of which it is to be explained. . . . Wherever we even just ask for an explanation there can no longer be a pure (absolutely free and self-dependent) self; for all explanation makes dependent.[17]

Schelling expressed the modern human awareness of autonomous being in the words: "I am because I am. This truth seizes hold, all of a sudden, of everyone."[18] Here in this credo of modern atheism we see the ultimate affirmation of the sense of self-mastery of human being over against the passivity of the religious consciousness. The split between philosophy and religion is now complete.

It remained for Ludwig Feuerbach to do a detailed critique of the Christian understanding of the givenness of life. Feuerbach, who was an atheist with a peculiar fascination for Christian theology, stated as his principal aim: to change

the friends of God into friends of man, believers into thinkers, worshippers into workers, candidates for the other world into students of this world, Christians who on their own confession are half-animal and half-angel, into men—whole men.[19]

Feuerbach's argument hinged on the simple assertion that humankind, which has the power to think and feel the infinite, wrongly attributes this infinity to God instead of seeing it as an attribute of human being:

If thou thinkest the infinite, thou perceivest and affirmest the infinitude of the power of thought; if thou feelest the infinite, thou feelest and affirmest the infinitude of the power of feeling.[20]

This line of reasoning, which is a reversal of the ontological argument for the existence of God that brought Anselm to worship, led to Feuerbach's primary criticism of religion and worship: "To enrich God, man must become poor; that God may be all, man must be nothing."[21] Here the religious affirmation of the givenness of life by God has been turned into its opposite—that God robs humankind of their freedom and responsibility for living.

Feuerbach's criticism of religion became the basis for the momentous attack on religion that was to follow by Karl Marx.

Religion is the sigh of the oppressed creature, the heart of a heartless world, just as it is the spirit of a spiritless situation. It is the *opium* of the people. The abolition of religion as the *illusory* happiness of the people is required for their *real* happiness. The demand to give up the illusions about its condition is the *demand to give up a condition which needs illusions.*[22]

Marx took Feuerbach's criticism of religion out of the theoretical realm into the practical. The rejection of religion becomes the beginning of revolution: "Once the earthly family is discovered to be the secret of the holy family, the form must then itself be criticized in theory and revolutionized in practice."[23] With Marx the dissolution of the relationship between religion and philosophy is confirmed. But philosophy itself comes under criticism in the name of a humanity that is taking charge of its own destiny, not only in thought, as the idealists would have it, but in practice. And so Marx makes his famous criticism of philosophy: "The philosophers have only interpreted the world, in various ways; the point however is to change it."[24]

This call for the exercise of human power, as numerous theologians of the twentieth century have noted, is not foreign to an attitude of faith that can be discerned in the Hebrew prophets and in the Christian understanding of God's call to participate in God's saving activity in the world. Looking at the essentially otherworldly religion of his day, Marx could not discern any empowerment for the exercise of human responsibility in the world. Religion stood for permanence and not change, for passivity, not freedom. Marx's criticism is not unlike the early Christian opposition to the temple cult and the observance of the Jewish law—with a significant difference.

Marx can be seen as the culminating figure in a process in philosophy that championed freedom over against the authority of metaphysics and religion as practiced by the church. But the modern concept of freedom as freedom from authority does not correspond with the Christian notion of freedom grounded in the authority of God's Word. Freedom can be consistent with worship of such a God, as my previous examination of worship in the New

Testament has indicated. Marx, in the interests of freedom, saw it as necessary to repudiate religion and worship, although it may be acknowledged, as some do, that Marx granted a limited value to religion in speaking of it as the "opium" that lifts the people's spirit in their state of oppression. Such a view, however, does not grant to religion and worship any capacity to empower people to bring about change in their living conditions. The drug-induced change of consciousness creates only the illusion of change. The psychological critique of religion by Sigmund Freud perceived religion also as an illusion, and, like Marx, Freud was influenced by the writings of Feuerbach. His use of the concept of "projection" in his analysis of religion can be traced to Feuerbach, who, as we have seen, regarded all the attributes ascribed to God in religion as really belonging to humankind. The separation of the sacred and profane in the secular attitude, as represented by Marx and Freud, is overcome simply by abolishing the former as a mere illusion.

The early Christians, however, made a metaphorical shift that enabled them to use the words and ritual actions of the cult with reference both to worship and to daily life. Now instead of directing the worshiper's gaze to a world beyond, the metaphor enabled the worshiper to participate in this world in a new way. The "as though not" of metaphor allowed for a response in the world other than what the powers-that-be called for. Worship as a metaphor of the dawning rule of God provided a motivation and empowerment for participating with God in overturning the current world, now seen as rapidly passing away. Far from standing for passivity or permanence in the world, this worship, as a celebration of freedom, opened the way to revolutionary change.

Marx's criticism of religion, however, in keeping with Feuerbach's, was grounded in a rejection of this capacity of metaphor. Symbol or metaphor for Feuerbach stood for a false view of transcendence that had to be rejected if human beings were to recover the attributes and values hitherto projected on God that rightly belonged to them. And so Feuerbach rejected the capacity of symbols or metaphors to point to any significance or mystery that transcends their natural qualities. He sought, as he said, to "put in the place of the barren baptismal water, the beneficial effect of real water."[25]

This "literalism" of Marx and Feuerbach that rejects metaphorical language is closely associated with, if it does not account for, the loss of transcendence that makes worship impossible for many in the post-Enlightenment era. We may consider, too, whether without the transcendence of metaphors, with their power to point beyond the status quo, any genuinely revolutionary change is possible, contrary to Marx's expectation. In chapter 5 I will examine the effects of the loss of transcendence on the worship of the church and the various efforts to recover it. The critical question for our age is whether transcendence can be recovered in a way that empowers for freedom rather than, as in its traditional form, reduces humankind to passivity.

5

The Loss of Transcendence

The growth of awareness of autonomy of the human being in Enlightenment philosophy emerged as an attack on the faith and doctrines of the church and, consequently, as a tremendous challenge to the church's worship in the era after the Enlightenment. It is possible, and indeed necessary, to see the life of the church since the eighteenth century, up to and including the present, as conditioned by the secular outlook of the Enlightenment. This can be said despite the fact that many people in the church accepted the view of the world as secular while seeking to maintain the church as a bastion of religion within a secular world. Atheists could then be regarded by Christians as suspect in both faith and morals, and therefore not to be associated with. Writing in 1970, Langdon Gilkey, in *Naming the Whirlwind*, challenged the church to recognize the secularity of its own outlook. This was after an explicit atheism had entered into Christian theology under the caption "Death of God," a famous phrase coined by Friedrich Nietzsche, an atheist philosopher of the previous century.

Gilkey characterized the secular outlook as a turning away from worlds beyond to this world of nature and history. If worship has to do with a sacred world beyond this one, then it appears that there is no continuing place for worship in the secular world. It is this separate sacred sphere that, according to Gilkey, is no longer accepted. The secular outlook

rejects any peculiarly religious means of knowing reality, be it called revelation or religious experience, and thus which finds meaningless or undiscoverable any category of the transcendent, the sacred, the holy, that which is more than the finite realities experienced in our ordinary secular contact with nature and with other persons in community.[1]

But it is precisely within these finite realities that Gilkey looked for a new experience of the sacred that can provide a basis for talking about and worshiping God. His theological concern is just one example of something that has been happening in the human sciences, art, and literature and in the daily experiences of many people both inside and outside the churches. It can be referred to as the loss and recovery of transcendence. This phenomenon is a prime factor in understanding what is happening in Christian worship in the era after the Enlightenment. In this chapter I shall look at the loss of transcendence and how this affected worship in the churches, before proceeding to look at the recovery of transcendence in chapter 6.

Many people in the nineteenth century mourned the passing of God, or faith in God, from the scene. The English poet Matthew Arnold, in his poem *Dover Beach*, caught the mood of sadness, and even fear, of his time as he depicted faith ebbing away like the tide, ending in a dark vision of a world in which "ignorant armies clash by night." Earlier Samuel Taylor Coleridge had responded in a more positive and orthodox fashion, having come into contact with the latest Enlightenment thinking during his travels on the Continent. In a personal copy of a book by Schelling from which I quoted earlier, Coleridge responded to Schelling's confident assertion: "I am because I am. This truth seizes hold all of a sudden, of everyone," by affirming with equal confidence: *"Jeden?"* "Everyone? I doubt it. Many may say: I am because God made me."[2]

Coleridge's friend Wordsworth took a dimmer view of what he perceived to be a loss of transcendence. In his *Ode on the Intimations of Immortality from Recollections of Early Childhood* he remembers the child's experience of nature as enveloped in a "celestial light" that then gradually "fades into the light of common day." Wordsworth attributed this loss in no small measure to modern education with its reasonable and commonsense approach to things. Nor was religious ceremony perceived by him as sufficient. Although he can be associated with the high church movement in the Church of England that sought to recover the sacramental nature of worship, he clearly found the primary source of a renewed sense of God's presence or the sacred apart from the worship of the church by communing with nature. The child and youth, with their clearer perception of, and joy in, the divine light in nature, have qualifications to be "Nature's priests."

To many of the Romantics, the dogmas and rituals of the institutional church were regarded as repressive and deadening to the religious spirit. William Blake sought transcendence in the inner being. He revealed his views of the church and its ritual in a little poem entitled "The Garden of Love."

> I went to the Garden of Love,
> And saw what I never had seen:
> A chapel was built in the midst,
> Where I used to play on the green.
>
> And the gates of this chapel were shut,
> And "Thou shalt not" writ over the door;
> So I turned to the Garden of Love,
> That so many sweet flowers bore:
>
> And I saw it was filled with graves,
> And tombstones where flowers should be;
> And priests in black gowns were walking their rounds,
> And binding with briars my joys and desires.

In New England at this time an extraecclesial religious awareness was being affirmed by the "Transcendentalists," such as Hawthorne, Emerson, and Thoreau. They were getting some of their inspiration from an acquaintance with Eastern philosophy and religion. The effort to emulate the wisdom of the East can be seen in Thoreau's cultivation of a writing style that made use of short pithy sayings: "Time is but the stream I go a-fishing in. I drink at it; but while I drink I see the sandy bottom and detect how shallow it is. Its thin current slides away, but eternity remains."[3] Here is an expression of a higher spirituality, as Thoreau believed, than can be realized in religious ritual.

Friedrich Schleiermacher is generally regarded as the first Christian theologian to respond to the challenge of the Enlightenment. As a young man thoroughly emersed in the secular society of Berlin at the beginning of the nineteenth century, he addressed his friends and peers in a brashly written book titled *Religion: Speeches to Its Cultured Despisers*. He shared their rejection of the rationalism of the philosophical tradition and the supernaturalism of the dogmatic tradition as these had been called into question by Kant. But he wanted to show these modern skeptics of religion that within their own experience there was an original "sense and taste for the Infinite"[4] that attested to the reality of God.

It was Schleiermacher's belief that the traditional supernaturalistic heritage, with its God who miraculously intervenes in events that can be objectively discerned and its worship that requires the mediation of priests between the divine and the human, was rightly denied. But Christian faith and worship, he maintained, could be affirmed on a different basis. "For," as he wrote to his friend Dr. Lücke, "where God has been rejected among us, it has always been the prevailing presentation that was meant rather than the idea itself."[5] And so over against the God of reason in traditional metaphysics and the supernaturalism of the dogmatic and liturgical tradition he sought to give theology a "province of its own," not in the moral will, as Kant maintained, but in an original instinct that he called "piety" or "feeling." In this respect he was taking seriously the Enlightenment discovery of religion as a historical and human phenomenon. Theology, then, became for Schleiermacher a descriptive science with its own subject matter. As he announced at the beginning of his mature work, *The Christian Faith*, he would offer a description of faith or piety as it is given in the Christian churches. Faith for Schleiermacher was a living relation to God rather than adherence to doctrine. He described this relationship as a "feeling of absolute dependence."[6] This feeling is not a description of one part of experience besides others, but refers to the "fundamental relation which must include all others in itself."[7] God is "the *Whence* of our receptive and active existence."[8]

By giving, as it were, a pointer to God rather than an objective account, Schleiermacher was seeking to avoid Kant's critique of objective language about God. Language about God is not directly based on objective knowledge, as is our language about things in this world. "None of the attributes which we ascribe to God is meant to designate something specific in God," but rather to "designate something special in the manner in which the feeling of absolute dependence is to be related to Him."[9] The language of the church, therefore, is always metaphorical. In this regard

Schleiermacher took special note of the hymns that Christians sing in worship, and of religious poetry. These metaphorical or symbolic representations, he noted, were taken over into philosophy, contrary to their original intention, and became natural theology.[10] What was ascribed to God metaphorically became speculations about qualities directly attributable to God.

We have considered Schleiermacher's contribution in some detail because of the importance of many of his concerns for subsequent developments in theology and worship. To his lasting credit Schleiermacher pointed the way to speaking about God in relation to the whole of life instead of to a separate sacred sphere. Already in his theology one can discern a beginning attempt to speak of the sacred not as a separate sphere apart from ordinary finite existence, but as a dimension of ordinary experience. God as "the *Whence* of our receptive and active existence" is related not only to the passive side of human experience, as in the usual religious outlook, but also to human strength and freedom. The exercise of that freedom no longer needs to be a threat to Christian faith and worship. Furthermore, by his insight into the nature of theological language—that it does not "designate something specific in God," but refers to the relationship between God and humanity— Schleiermacher had overcome the objection that Feuerbach was later to make against Christian theology: that it projects on God attributes that rightly belong only to human beings. If Freud had taken his cue from Schleiermacher instead of from Feuerbach, the history of modern psychology might have been different. Finally, Schleiermacher's insight into the metaphorical nature of theological language and worship was of immense significance for the later development of hermeneutics. including current attempts to develop a liturgical theology grounded in metaphor.

His use of the terms feeling and dependency, however, caused much confusion among succeeding theologians who continued to understand them with reference to partial aspects of human experience. Rudolph Otto, in his *The Idea of the Holy*, substituted the word creature-feeling for Schleiermacher's "feeling of absolute dependence" in order to indicate its "immediate and primary reference to an object outside the self." "There must be felt a something numinous,"[11] said Otto. With this psychologizing approach Otto undid Schleiermacher's insistence on the metaphorical nature of language about God by substituting for it a direct experience of God. He also reverted back to regarding religious feeling as a partial aspect of human experience, rather than as an attitude that accompanies all experience. And so he contrasted the sense of *mysterium tremendum* in religious experience with the "profane, non-religious mood of everyday experience."[12] Religious consciousness is once again cut off from secular experience, and worship is seen as belonging to a separate sacred sphere.

A danger in Schleiermacher's attempt to find some point of contact with a secular age by looking for the reality of God and the sacred in ordinary experience was the loss of these realities by a simple unmetaphorical identification of them with realities in nature and history. The divine would become nothing more than a designation for the highest and best in ordinary existence as perceived by any given culture. This was the conclusion, indeed, to which Feuerbach had come. With his affirmation of a "wholly other" God, Otto sought to overcome what he perceived as this major flaw in the liberal theology following Schleiermacher. Liberal theology, as it was called among Protestants, and, to some extent, Modernism among Roman Catholics, tended to eschew the traditional rites and dogmas of the church in favor of individual religious experience. Instead of talking about the divinity of God, they looked for the divinity in humanity. They preferred to regard Jesus as an exemplary moral teacher rather than as the Christ of doctrine. The Sermon on the Mount became their canon of scripture as opposed to the letters of Paul, which were regarded as a perversion of the simple religion of Jesus. The doctrine of the Holy Spirit gave way to talk about human spirituality.

Where worship was still an accepted practice for liberals it was valued for its salutary effects on morals rather than as a sheer act of praise. Preaching was important as an occasion for teaching religious truths and inculcating higher values. The sacraments were seen, not as God's action, but as human actions that elevate the mind and soul to a higher spiritual level. Worship, therefore, was more readily understood as a form of empowerment than as an act of praise, although some would agree that praise, with its implied humility, is also good for the soul if not carried to extremes.

The question that, in this century, was put to this liberal attempt at accommodation with the age (preeminently by Karl Barth) was whether the liberals had not lost the substance and reality of the Christian faith, including the "wholly other" God. Had they not, indeed, become proponents of a mere cultural religion that enshrined the highest values to which the culture could attain? Barth, significantly, came to this view when, as a young pastor of a church in Safenwil, Switzerland, he discerned the discrepancy between what was being affirmed about God in worship and what he had been taught by his liberal teachers.

In speaking of liberalism we are referring to a phenomenon of reaction to the Enlightenment and its impact on religion. Beside liberalism, and a continuing factor in the nineteenth and twentieth centuries, but with roots in pre-Enlightenment Europe, was the vigorous expression of religion known as evangelical Christianity. Evangelicalism emerged in the eighteenth century in Germany as an outgrowth of pietism and in England in the movement associated with the names of John and Charles Wesley. It quickly spread to North America, where it became primarily identified with revivalism, although major denominations such as The United Methodist Church in the USA and The United Church of Canada can claim it as their heritage.

Although one cannot begin to comprehend the wealth and breadth of this seemingly spontaneous upsurge of religious faith, one can point to some of its characteristics as they pertain to worship and the life of the Christian in the world. One can identify as a watchword of the movement the word salvation, and discern its scope, as beginning in the individual and extending to comprehend the whole world. Its zeal for the salvation of the individual as something identifiable within the individual's own experience, and its worldwide vision issued in a strong missionary thrust and emphasis on conversion. Conversion referred to the change of heart whereby a person becomes a Christian, but also referred to the process of growth toward the promised perfection known as sanctification. What is clearly envisaged here is the New Testament ideal of a holy people, as opposed to a cult with holy priests. This holiness extended beyond the sphere of worship into the living of an upright and moral life in the world.

In worship, occasions had to be allowed for appeal to the experience of the sacred, with opportunities for individual expression of commitment. The Wesleys, who intended their efforts to be a reform of life and worship in the established Church of England, saw the recovery of the sacraments, particularly the Eucharist, as a way of celebrating evangelical faith and commitment. When this aim was frustrated by the rejection of the new movement by the established church, other ways of expressing commitment assumed primary importance, including the altar call, testimonials, and the weekly midweek prayer meetings. What took the place of a symbolic ritual that unified the hearts and minds of the people in worship was no doubt the singing of hymns, for which the movement was especially known.

In these hymns, many of which were composed by John and Charles Wesley, can be discerned the distinctive qualities of evangelical faith and experience. Nothing is so evident in this singing as the confidence of faith, which I have already identified as the chief characteristic of the transformed worship of the early Christians.

> Jesus, united by Thy grace
> And each to each endeared,
> With confidence we seek Thy face,
> And know our prayer is heard.

What prevents this confidence from becoming complacent is the characteristic zeal and longing for perfection, experienced as an intimate relationship to God, as in this hymn by the German evangelical Count von Zinzendorf, translated by John Wesley:

> O Thou, to whose all-searching sight
> The darkness shineth as the light,
> Search, prove my heart; it pants for Thee;
> O burst these bonds, and set it free!

The connection between the experience of salvation and empowerment for service in the world is expressed in Charles Wesley's well-known hymn "A Charge to Keep I Have." Verse two goes:

> To serve the present age,
> My calling to fulfill,—

O may it all my powers engage
To do my Master's will.

Although evangelical Christianity had its roots in pre-Enlightenment times, and with its emphasis on experience may even have
been a precursor of the Enlightenment, it did not remain un-
affected by the strong challenge put to religion by the atheistic
philosophy of the Enlightenment. In the nineteenth century it
became closely associated with the post-Enlightenment phenomenon known as fundamentalism. Fundamentalism emerged as a
reaction to the pressure of the secularity of the age by withdrawing
into the unassailable realm of private experience bolstered by an
appeal to an infallible scripture, interpreted literalistically. Fundamentalists perceived in Darwin's theory of the evolution of species
a threat both to their special dignity as creatures of God and to the
Bible as divine revelation. They also vigorously opposed the work
of the biblical critics (known as higher criticism) for its reduction of
the Bible to a human book of myth and history instead of a work of
divine inspiration. By so doing they closed the door to the one
route that could have enabled a positive response to Darwin's
theory by affirming the Genesis stories of creation, not as a factual
account of the beginning of the world, but as myths depicting the
continuing relationship between creature and Creator.

The agony that the perceived conflict between faith and modern science inflicted on the early fundamentalists is nowhere depicted more poignantly than in Edmund Gosse's book *Father and
Son*.[13] The book describes the struggle of the father, the paleon-
tologist Philip Gosse, to accommodate his discoveries of the bones
of primitive creatures with the fundamentalist beliefs of his
Plymouth Brethren church. After much soul-searching Gosse con-
cluded, to the astonishment or amusement of his peers, that God
created the world exactly as the Genesis account gives it, complete
with the bones of dinosaurs. Named the "Omphalos" theory, with
reference to its implication that Adam and Eve would have had
belly buttons, although having no need of them, it was quickly
seen by unfriendly assailants to imply that God must have placed
these paleolithic remains in the earth as a test of faith for people
who would be tempted by them to doubt divine revelation. Gosse's

ingenious solution was the sad product of a sacrifice of the intellect—surely one of the most dehumanizing demands a sacrificial religion can make! This is extreme Protestantism's unritualistic version of sacrificial religion.

What can elicit our sympathy, even pity, for the pain and weaknesses of an earlier age becomes harder to accept near the end of the twentieth century, when fundamentalism is experiencing a resurgence and its advocates are asking that "creation science" be taught beside evolution in the schools. The danger of their belittling of human powers becomes frighteningly evident when we hear television evangelists, from a literal reading of the book of Revelation, associating the threat of nuclear war with the Battle of Armageddon, which must come in order to usher in the final age of peace. This makes them part of a small but exceedingly dangerous group of people who are actually looking forward to nuclear war!

With all their efforts to establish a bulwark between themselves and the secularity of the modern age, the fundamentalists can be understood as essentially a modern phenomenon. Their literalistic interpretation of the scriptures has much in common with the reliance on experiential knowledge and concern for facts (as opposed to metaphors) of the prevailing secular attitude. No one was more fundamentalist than the atheistic Feuerbach or Marx, with their rejection of the capacity of symbols or metaphors to point to any significance or mystery that transcends their natural qualities. One can also detect a spiritual kinship between this literalistic outlook and the attitude of some earlier biblical scholars, whose preoccupation with objective historical research was often at the expense of the spiritual and metaphorical meaning of the texts. This reduction of reality to the factual has had an impoverishing effect in many areas of modern life, including the worship of the church. Indeed a rejection of metaphor, as seen with Marx, makes worship as praise and empowerment impossible.

A more positive response to the secularity of the age, which sought a renewal of worship by recovering the mystery and beauty of the worship of an earlier age, was the movement in England variously known as ritualism, Anglo-Catholicism, Tractarianism, the Oxford movement, or simply High Church. This liturgical trend, with its parallels in the pre-Raphaelite movement and the

Cambridge movement for Gothic revival in the arts and architecture, had a genuine concern not merely for decorative and imitative values, but for recovering the true spirit of an earlier age of faith. This concern for authenticity caused some of the leaders of the movement, including Newman in theology and Pugin in architecture, to seek their spiritual home in the Church of Rome.

John Henry Newman, who later became a cardinal in the Roman Church, gave an account of the spiritual struggles he went through before deciding to leave the Church of England in his *Apologia Pro Vita Sua*, which has become a classic of spiritual writing. Newman, like Matthew Arnold, had a profoundly troubled view of the current condition of humankind as "having no hope, and without God in the world,"[14] a result, as he saw it, of the "all-corroding, all-dissolving skepticism of the intellect."[15] Coupled with this pessimism about reason were memories of childhood's mystical sense of God's immediate presence and the transparency of the material world to the spiritual. But unlike Wordsworth, who looked to nature for transcendence, he found in the sacramental system of the church "the fine perception of that subtle and mysterious analogy which exists between the physical and moral world; which makes outward things and qualities the natural types and emblems of inward gifts and emotions."[16] This quotation, applied to Newman by a contemporary, originally referred to the essence of poetry but could also serve as a fine description of the sacramental universe of the Middle Ages that Newman sought to recover.

In view of the authenticity of the religious experience of many in the high church movement, including Newman, not too much irony must be seen in the coincidence that at the very time when Darwin's *Origin of Species* was emerging as a perceived threat to faith and human dignity, the established church was debating in the House of Lords the issue pertaining to the "Ornaments Rubric" in the *Book of Common Prayer*. What began, however, as a serious attempt to establish "true principles" for worship over a situation that appeared to be leading to disintegration, gradually itself deteriorated. In the Victorian age it became increasingly an aesthetic concern for a "churchly style" in ritual and architecture that was based on an imitation of earlier styles. This trend eventually broadened to include the so-called nonliturgical churches, which were building pseudo-Gothic churches and remodeling church sanctuaries from central pulpit to split chancels as late as the midtwentieth century. This imitation not only fostered an unrealism in worship, but also perpetuated a split between the sacred values of worship and those of the secular world.

Of the high church movement itself it can be said that the genuineness of its original concern for the reform of worship has made it, in many respects, a leader, along with the liturgical movement in the Roman Catholic Church that culminated in Vatican II, in the twentieth-century liturgical movement, particularly with respect to the recovery of earlier forms of worship reaching back to the earliest period of church history. Its value has been severely restricted, however, by its failure to address the challenge of the Enlightenment to the authority and sacramentalism of an earlier age, or what Louis Weil has called "the inherited liturgical mentality."[17] This sacramental piety, as he points out, takes the form of purely privatized acts of devotion cut off from the wider sphere of human existence. Weil can point to some noteworthy early thrusts to the contrary in the high church movement, in which the corporate reality of the church was reaffirmed and the liturgy was seen in its proper connection with the church's ministry among the poor. Nevertheless he acknowledges that the individualized liturgical piety has tended to predominate. "If we want to understand the social consequences of the Eucharist," he writes, "what is required is a radical conversion, a cleansing of the inherited liturgical mentality."[18]

This call for genuine reform can be properly addressed not to one tradition only, but to the liturgical movement among all the churches, which is always in danger of becoming merely a matter of repristination rather than renewal. Worship in the nineteenth century largely existed at some distance from the emerging modern world. It can continue as something precious to a few but not as an option for those who are striving for a more open encounter with the spirit and concerns of the age.

But before leaving the nineteenth century I need to acknowledge that Christianity was not without a significant achievement that grew out of its concern for the betterment of the human condition. This concern was exhibited by some as a concern for a higher standard of personal morality (holiness) in one's occupation and private life. For others it issued in a call for remedial social action in the world. Christians indeed were in the forefront of many movements of social reform. The stories of these achievements are well known. They include the work of Robert Raikes in founding the Sunday school movement as a means of educating children who were caught in the labor force of the early Industrial Age. William Wilberforce and Abraham Lincoln are remembered for their opposition to slavery; Dr. Wilfred Grenfell, for his medical work with the native people of the Labrador coast; and Nellie McClung, for championing women's rights and the temperance movement in Canada.

Possibly the most notable social achievements on this continent are associated with the Social Gospel movement, which got its name and theoretical basis from the theology of Walter Rauschenbusch. It was closely allied with the growth of the modern labor movements, but its concerns extended to such issues and areas as urban poverty, women's suffrage, immigration, pacifism, and home and foreign missions. The Social Gospel movement was not generally antagonistic to worship. Indeed many of its leaders found the worshiping community hostile to their concerns and were driven out of the church into politics and other fields. There was even the effort in Winnipeg, Canada, at the time of the general strike in 1919 to form a Labour Church whose worship mainly consisted of preaching about the new program to change society. This did not last long. Some joined the Communist party. Others in Canada were active in forming a new political party of the left called the Cooperative Commonwealth Federation. This socialist party and its successor, the New Democratic Party, have made an immense contribution to social justice and welfare in Canadian life.

It has to be said of the Social Gospelers, however, that their interest in worship was, at most, peripheral to their concern for social change. They were more interested in service than in symbol, in instrumental programs than in sacraments. This, of course, is hardly surprising, given the separation between worship and social action they found in the churches of their time. No one regarded worship, with its privatistic and otherworldly orientation and passive tendencies, as much of a force for social change in this world.

I have reviewed in brief various reactions among Christians of the nineteenth century to the challenge to worship put by the Enlightenment with its rejection of transcendence as it had traditionally been understood and experienced. The outcome appears to be that worship remained cut off from secular life, and thus was a preoccupation of a diminishing number of people. The more vigorous and successful developments in Christianity were in areas other than worship, such as in mission and social action. And often because the social commitment remained separate from the worship of the church, it could be no more than a partial concern of people within the churches, somewhat at variance with other churchly concerns.

There was and remains, moreover, an area of modern life that the social commitment of the churches has left untouched. There is a longing among people both inside and outside of the churches for a recovery of the mystery in life that was lost to the secular age, with its reduction of mystery to problems to be solved by modern technology. There is also an alienation in modern life that scientific knowledge and social and political programs, including that of Marxism, are powerless to address. The recovery of transcendence within and not separate from secular life remains a pressing concern in a secular age. That is, it must be found not only in relation to the passivity of life, but also where humankind acts, or seeks to act, in freedom and strength.

6

The Recovery of Transcendence

The exploration of the recovery of transcendence in this chapter begins with the story of Dietrich Bonhoeffer, one of the first people within the church in this century to recognize the secularity of the world's outlook and to seek to embrace it in the church. Many people misunderstand his motives and thinking as a symptom or even as a cause of the decline of worship and the loss of transcendence in the latter half of the twentieth century. But, as I hope to show, Bonhoeffer provided a new basis for recovering transcendence after the loss of the old, and with it new possibilities for worship as praise and empowerment that remain only partially realized.

Bonhoeffer's story is well known. He was a pastor and theologian of the Evangelical (Lutheran) Church in Germany before and during World War II. Imprisoned by the Nazis for an attempt on Hitler's life, he was hanged after about two years in captivity. His letters from prison, gathered in *Letters and Papers from Prison*, startled the world by what they said about the new shape of Christianity in the modern world. Much of what was subsequently written by theologians about secularization stemmed from some brief comments he made in his letters.

He made this surprising thesis: "We are moving towards a completely religionless time; people as they are now simply cannot be religious anymore."[1] This movement toward a nonreligious world had been developing, he maintained, for several centuries. He called it the "coming of age" of humanity. Human beings now are autonomous in all areas of life; that is, they can deal with all questions without "recourse to God as a working hypothesis."[2] "It is becoming evident," he wrote, "that everything gets along without 'God'—and, in fact, just as well as before."³ The reaction of the church to this fact, Bonhoeffer believed, was to see it as a great defection from God and to oppose it by bringing God and Christ back into the picture, trying to prove that the world cannot get along without God. Some matters are reserved for God, such as those areas of life in which human weakness can be discerned—death, guilt, unresolved problems, and so on. But this is merely to resort to a "god of the gaps," said Bonhoeffer. This attack on the "adulthood" of the world is "pointless, ignoble and un-Christian."⁴ It is a "revolt of inferiority."⁵

Bonhoeffer's solution was to say that people must stop trying to find a place for God in a world that knows itself to be godless. By "godless world" he meant one that was de-divinized and, therefore, free of idols. This is a promising godlessness because it provides an occasion for affirming Christ at the center of life rather than at its edges. He wrote:

Here again, God is no stop-gap; he must be recognized at the centre of life, not when we are at the end of our resources; it is his will to be recognized in life, and not only when death comes; in health and vigour, and not only in suffering; in our activities, and not only in sin. The ground for this lies in the revelation of God in Jesus Christ.⁶

Bonhoeffer, in this passage, is echoing Schleiermacher's view of God as the Whence of both our passive and active existence, and Paul's embracing of the whole of life as an expression of Christian freedom. Bonhoeffer spelled out what he meant by this incarnational view of God in Christ at the center of life in an important letter of July 16, 1944. In it he reverses the usual religious expectation by depicting a God who comes not in strength, but in weakness. Taking up the theme of living without God, that is, without any appeal to the power of God in the world to supplement human weakness, he wrote:

And we cannot be honest unless we recognize that we have to live in the world *etsi deus non daretur.* And this is just what we do recognize—before God! God himself compels us to recognize it. So our coming of age leads us to a true recognition of our situation before God. God would have us know that we must live as men who manage our lives without him. The God who is with us is the God who forsakes us (Mark 15.34). The God who lets us live in the world without the working hypothesis of God is the God before whom we stand continually. Before God and with God we live without God. God lets himself be pushed out of the world on to the cross. He is weak and powerless in the world, and that is precisely the way, the only way, in which he is with us and helps us. . . .

Here is the decisive difference between Christianity and all religions. Man's religiosity makes him look in his distress to the power of God in the world: God is the *deus ex machina*. The Bible directs man to God's powerlessness and suffering; only the suffering God can help.[7]

What, therefore, is transcendence for Bonhoeffer? It is not reaching out in our weakness to the power of God or taking refuge in a world beyond. It is rather experienced in worldly living—in living with God where God is to be found in this world. "Worldly" life means to "share in God's sufferings," or as the disciples were called on to do, "watching with Christ in Gethsemane."[8] Transcendence then can be described as "existence for others"[9] or reaching out to the neighbor.

All this is now familiar stuff in theological circles. It has been quoted innumerable times but mainly in the interests of those who were developing a secular theology. The theme of secularization now feels rather remote at a time when religion seems to have been making a comeback. Bonhoeffer's prediction of a time of "no religion at all" now looks like a wrong prognosis. So his ideas on transcendence have not been picked up to any great extent by theologians and others seeking a recovery of transcendence. His phrase "the beyond in the midst,"[10] it is true, has supported an approach to the sacred not apart from secular life, but in it. His rejection of "thinking in terms of two spheres"[11] has given impetus to the attacks on the dualism inherent in Christian faith, which is charged with being responsible for everything from the world-denying religiosity of some Christian worship to the reality-diminishing sterility of the secular age.

What had not been picked up from Bonhoeffer in the secular period was the paradox in Bonhoeffer's view of transcendence: that it can be recovered *only by abandoning the search*. It is worth going back to Bonhoeffer to recover this insight, which has great implications for worship in its relationship to ordinary experience.

To understand what this paradox could mean one has to recall what Bonhoeffer meant by religion. He was using an insight he had acquired from Karl Barth, who had attacked religion as being the antithesis of faith. Religion, in Barth's view, is humankind's search for God. Where it conflicts with faith is in its failure to recognize or to accept that God searches for us and has, moreover, entered into our worldly existence in Jesus Christ.

Worship, therefore, can never be a means of approaching God, who dwells remote from human life. It is transformed by faith into a celebration of God's coming. And this celebration can only happen authentically in the midst of life, where Christ is to be found.

One immediately senses the contrast with this on examining the literature of transcendence that emerged after the secular period. Michael Novak's *Ascent of the Mountain, Flight of the Dove*[12] used the motif of a search—a religious drive that pushes the earnest seeker ever upward in an ascending scale of standpoints to new visions of reality. This search picked up momentum throughout the seventies in a great upsurge of religion—occult sciences, witchcraft, demonology, drug cults, I Ching, Eastern mysticism, Jesus people, etc.—prompting the comment "God may have died in the sixties . . . but with the seventies gods and devils rise anew."[13] The chief characteristic of this religious quest was a focus on experience as consciousness-raising, as heightened awareness, in order to discern the transcendent dimensions of life. Sacred reality is understood as always present and surrounding us. If our perception is altered, we can discern its presence. The question that has to be asked concerning Christian worship is whether faith is simply altered perception, or does it have to do with a *new reality?*

The literature of transcendence crossed a number of different disciplines—anthropology, psychology, theology—and concerned itself with such aspects of contemporary life as drug experience, the ecology crisis and accompanying disillusionment with technology, and the recovery of a sense of religious wonder. Its attractiveness to many people, including many Christians, was its recognition of, and its attempts to overcome, the deep-rooted alienation that afflicts our Western technological society at the level of both personal and institutional life.[14] It was not surprising that people began to seek out the roots of this alienation in the tradition from which they had come. Traditional Christianity consequently came under critical scrutiny, particularly the Christian conception of God.

What was thought to be lacking in the traditional faith in God was an awareness of the immediate presence of the divine in human experience. The notion of a Creator God elevated God above creation. It de-divinized the world—a phrase used earlier with reference to Bonhoeffer's theology. In this world where God dwells apart there is no call for a sense of wonder before the mystery of the divine in the reality that surrounds us. On this view it was hardly surprising that Christian theologians would come to speak of the "death of God." This rose out of their inability to experience the immediate presence of the Divine within the framework of traditional Christian symbols for God. Sam Keen, for instance, pointed out that it is the role of religious institutions to be "responsive to the experience of the sacred."[15] He went on to account for the fact that many people were bypassing these institutions in their search for transcendence: "If they [the institutions] have become irrelevant it is not because they are institutions but because they have been unresponsive to the growing edge of the awareness of the sacred."[16]

For those who began to search elsewhere for the sacred, instead of looking for it in the dualistic framework that separates the natural world from the supernatural, the sacred from the profane, or God from humanity, the profane world (literally outside the temple), or the world of daily experience, became the place to look. There are not two worlds, in other words, but only one. But that one world is not without a sacred dimension. The word sacred, then, is not in fundamental opposition to the "secular," as has usually been thought. As Eugene H. Maly put it, "the word 'sacred' describes the relationship of the secular to the transcendent reality."[17]

Much of this is quite consistent with what we saw in the theologies of Schleiermacher and Bonhoeffer, both of whom started from a critical stance toward the traditional supernaturalist framework. The question, however, remains: What is identified as the sacred behind Christian worship?

Sam Keen, in his *Apology for Wonder,* differentiated the traditional from contemporary religious consciousness by distinguishing between worship and celebration:

The traditional religious mode of expressing gratitude is worship. . . . The religious consciousness is constituted by the movement of thought from the given to the Giver, from the contingent to the source or from the world to God.[18]

However, "if worship moves from symbol to a transcendent source, celebration consists of rejoicing in the presence of things."[19] Keen proceeded to point out that this "new search for immediacy . . . accounts for the growing interest in Zen and the exploration of techniques for awakening sensitivity."[20]

The contrast Keen was purportedly drawing was between the traditional and the contemporary religious consciousness. But had he not, in fact, drawn the line between Christian (and Jewish) worship and other expressions of religiosity? As seen in the earlier examination of biblical religion, the Hebrews believed in a God who transcends nature and the cosmos, but whose revelation is embodied in particular historical events. *YHWH*, therefore, is a God who, in particular times and places, *acts*, and in this action calls for a response of faith. Such a God cannot, as could a cosmic principle or a "sacred dimension of reality," be comprehended directly by the enlightened reason or heightened consciousness. Nor could God be joined by sacred rites that symbolize and make efficaciously available the elemental powers that surround and profoundly affect human existence. Such religious means of bridging the gap between human beings and God are no longer necessary with a God who comes.

From such a God as *YHWH* one can expect something new in history rather than simply "rejoicing in the presence of things." Jesus preached the coming of God's reign as the future God has in store for the world. His followers came to see in Jesus a decisive action of God fulfilling all past actions and opening the way to the future. But they discovered this only after Jesus' crucifixion and resurrection, when he was about to leave them. They then took their bearings from the covenant he made with them in bread and wine that enjoined them to "proclaim the Lord's death until he comes." This mystery or sacrament was a celebration of a presence, to be sure, but the presence of the Crucified One, whose death calls them always out of the present, which is soon past and done with, toward a new future revealed in the resurrection. Jesus' disciples enter into that future by participating in Christ's suffering and death on the cross and in his resurrection, becoming, as Paul said, "a fellowship of his sufferings"; or having that quality of self-transcendence in their lives that Bonhoeffer identified as "existence for others."

In this new relationship of sharing, *koinonia* (the RSV translates this "communion"), the religious question of passivity or mastery no longer matters. As Paul says: "I know how to be abased, and I know how to abound; in any and all circumstances I have learned the secret of facing plenty and hunger, abundance and want. I can do all things in him who strengthens me [Phil. 4:12–13]." Yes, Paul looks to God for strength, but he finds it not, as the religious person would expect, in a power that transcends human weakness, but in the human weakness of One dying on a cross. There is no God above this world to whom we can appeal to overcome our weakness or supplement our strength. The only God we know is a "worldly" God whose strength is revealed in weakness.

As Christians we are called to participate in that worldly vulnerability in a life lived for others. We will find among those who have been made powerless and vulnerable by oppression, accident, and want signs of Christ's broken body in the world, and therefore we will seek *koinonia* with them as a way of being in fellowship with Christ. Indeed the poor of this world may be viewed by Christians as sacraments of Christ's presence. Christians are called to eat at the same table with them. For their part the poor will provide the right spirit for the meal. From our store of goods we can provide the sustenance with the bread and wine we bring. And together we can eat and drink in wonder and gratitude.

With the poor, of course, our worship will not be a rejoicing in the presence of things, as Keen suggests, for their life is characterized by want. Rather, it will be an expectant worship, a worship that joyfully anticipates a world in which there will be no more want and the oppressor will no longer hold sway. There is hope and joy in this worship because it already tastes that which is to come but is not yet fully realized. There is defiance in this worship because it refuses to acquiesce in the status quo and knows how to stare down the rulers of this world. There is forgiveness in this worship for it recognizes that the barriers that divide human beings—male and female, Christian and Jew and Hindu and Muslim, rich and poor, oppressor and oppressed—have no lasting power. These barriers will crumble, and all will eat and drink together at the heavenly table.

Indeed we can, in faith, begin to live *as though* these barriers were not there. This *as though not* of freedom can be realized only by stepping out boldly. Yes, enough of these barriers are left to hurt as we pass through them. Our flesh may be torn and our bodies broken even as Christ's body was broken. But we will accept that vulnerability, that brokenness, for the sake of love, for Christ's sake and in the hope of Christ's resurrection. This is what we mean when we break bread together and drink wine from one cup. The broken bread and shared cup are signs of the vulnerability and invincibility of this new life in Christ.

Because the reality that Christians worship is not simply *there* as a static presence, but always behind and before, having come and coming again, past and future, it is expressed only in metaphor, in word and symbol or sign-act. We shall have to explore more fully the function of words and symbols in Christian worship in future chapters but can begin by recalling that they serve the function of making present. It is a presence that implies a relationship of mutuality and participation in which a communication takes place. The normal human way of communicating is with words and gestures, or sign-acts. Christians believe that God chooses this way of communicating with us.

If we recall now the two kinds of prayer with which I began chapter 2 we are able to elaborate on the difference between the two. One was a silent rumination on the goodness of what is given—a rejoicing in the presence of things. The other involved words in an act of praise: "Blessed is the Lord our God, Maker of the Universe, who causes bread to come forth from the earth." This word prayer reaches beyond the current moment to remember other times, both good and bad, through which God's people have been delivered to this day that is hallowed in eating and drinking. With the words of blessing, the food and drink become metaphors of a covenant between God and the people God has chosen. Jesus used this covenant language when he ate and drank with his disciples. "This cup is the new covenant in my blood. Do this, as often as you drink it, in remembrance of me [1 Cor. 11:25]."

For this covenant, memory is important. Not simply the remembrance of events that are past and done with. But an act in which other times and places are drawn together in the current moment. The word for this kind of thankful remembering is anamnesis, which is the opposite of amnesia, or forgetting. "Anamnesis" is "not forgetting." There is a note of defiance in the negativity of this word, an "in spite of" or "nevertheless." Not everything is peace and harmony, as it is on Huxley's island, to be sure. But whatever the circumstances of this life, God and God's goodness, which is experienced as deliverance from want and oppression, *will be remembered*. It will be a specific memory of particular actions in history in which God has demonstrated a gracious will toward human beings, acts of deliverance, acts of healing, forgiving actions, and supremely the action of raising Jesus from the dead. This remembering is not possible, of course, only in our own power of remembering because we, like the people of Israel, who were often chastised by the prophets, are a forgetful people. We can only remember because God remembers,[21] and God comes to us always in Word as well as in Sacrament to jog our memories. Word and Sacrament, therefore, belong together.

Besides the remembering there is anticipation. With the "in spite of" there is a "not yet." Memory and hope. *Maranatha*, "Come, Lord Jesus," is an acclamation from early Christian worship. The people call on the Spirit to come, the Spirit that unites the church and will bind Christians with all other human beings in bonds of love, the Spirit that is the sign of the New Age. Again this calling on the Spirit is not possible without the Word of promise that instills hope in our hearts for Christ's coming. Christian prayer is both *anamnesis* and *epiclesis* (the calling on the Spirit). The

87

Christian community receives its identity from *anamnesis* as an act of praise. *Epiclesis* calls the church into being and empowers it for living.

But this language of praise and empowerment is not simply a timeless given to be learned by rote and repeated in any and all circumstances. The church has the task of learning its language of worship in every age—of discovering the metaphors that can embrace both eternity and time, present, past, and future. For this task the church must look to the scriptures and to the tradition of the church to learn the story that has been told of people's faith and God's doing in times past. It has to look, as Jesus did, to the events of the present day to learn the story that is unfolding in God's continuing plan and in the lives of the people now. And in the confluence of these stories it will see the opening to the future that God has in store for the whole world. The liturgy of the church is the rehearsal of these stories in word and sign-act.

As discussed earlier, the language of faith has undergone a radical upheaval in the modern age as a result of the loss of the traditional awareness of transcendence within a dualistic world view. Also noted was the thrust toward a new metaphorical language of faith in New Testament Christianity that issued in worship as a celebration of freedom. This new language that rejected the separation of the sacred and profane, supernatural and natural, law and freedom into two isolated and discrete realities was not completely successful in transforming the existing categories, and worship reverted back to the legalistic system of earlier cults, cut off from ordinary life. The result was a religion of authority. Worship was an instrument of maintaining a hierarchical order in society with clergy in control and laity in a position of passivity. Philosophy became the means of human growth toward the autonomy of reason, and freedom from external authority. And with Marx the movement culminated in a call for revolution to overcome the structures that perpetuate the authority relationships in society, including the worship of the church, which Marx saw as giving a divine sanction to these structures. In his rejection of religion Marx also denied the language of metaphor that points to the transcendent.

The church awaits, therefore, a new language of worship that overcomes the traditional dichotomies, which are experienced as alienating and debilitating to the exercise of human power and freedom. It will exhibit a new awareness of transcendence, not apart from ordinary life, but within it. This new language of transcendence will speak of the givenness of life, not in terms of passivity, but as an openness to and participation in the New Age of God's rule of justice and peace that is already dawning within a world in which the old structures of oppression are passing away.

Dietrich Bonhoeffer glimpsed such a vision of the rebirth of a Christian language of worship in which the word of God will be so uttered "that the world will be changed and renewed by it."[22] But he was no less certain that the heritage of religious language could no longer speak to the present age without radical change. In "Thoughts on Baptism," written for his nephew, he wrote:

Reconciliation and redemption, regeneration and the Holy Spirit, love of our enemies, cross and resurrection, life in Christ and Christian discipleship—all these things are so difficult and so remote that we hardly venture any more to speak of them.[23]

Speaking of the church in Germany during the war years, including the Confessing Church, he added:

Our church, which has been fighting in these years only for its self-preservation, as though that were an end in itself, is incapable of taking the word of reconciliation and redemption to mankind and the world. Our earlier words are therefore bound to lose their force and cease, and our being Christians today will be limited to two things: prayer and righteous action among men. All Christian thinking, speaking, and organizing must be born anew out of this prayer and action.[24]

Bonhoeffer was exploring the idea of a continuance of worship as an "arcane discipline," by which he seems to have meant at minimum a separation of Christian worship from the dominant religious expressions of the day. Privately it would mean continuing with the disciplines of prayer, meditation, and Bible reading that we know Bonhoeffer never abandoned throughout the ordeal of the last years of his life. But Christians would be known publicly, not by their ceremonies, but by their commitment with other people of good will to the cause of justice and peace in the world. Out of this commitment a rebirth of language would occur that would speak with power—a "language of a new righteousness and truth, proclaiming God's peace with men and the coming of his kingdom."[25]

Although this will be a new language, it will not be new merely in the sense of substituting one set of words and actions for another, a method that has been tried unsuccessfully by people who substitute "contemporary" for "traditional" worship. The early church accomplished a radical shift in its worshiping—a metaphorical transference of the language of the cult from the sacred realm to embrace the whole of life. So, too, the modern church will come once again to speak the traditional ritual language of word and sign-act with new meaning arising out of the authenticity of its life in the world. Already we can hear and see this renewed language in which Christians are engaged in the struggle for liberation and peace. This struggle is most apparent in the countries of the Third World, where worship is being transformed within the experience of small groups of Christians who call themselves "base communities." But it is occurring no less among the disadvantaged people of the affluent West—the poor, gays and lesbians, native peoples, women, and children. In an age when the exercise of human power is threatening our "fragile earth," as one eucharistic prayer puts it, there is a growing consciousness of our human interaction and mutuality with all creatures and the need to exercise care for the whole earth.

The worship of the mainstream churches of the affluent West is only beginning to be touched by this new sensitivity of struggle and caring. But there are signs of change—in the ordination of women among an increasing number of churches, in the beginning of acceptance of lesbians and gay men for ordained ministry, in the making of churches accessible to the disabled, in the inclusion of children and youth in worship, in the use of metaphors from conditions of life, such as poverty, oppression, and sickness, as well as health, prosperity, and freedom, that allow all people to feel included whatever their personal circumstances may be. As the churches come to participate more fully in the struggles of those who are on the periphery of society we can expect to hear different voices and see new faces in the worship assembly. And from these newcomers, these strangers in our midst, we will learn a language that has hitherto been unheard—a language that speaks of the vulnerability of the cross and the power of the resurrection.

7

The Power of Metaphor

George Orwell's epochal novel *1984*[1] depicts a nightmare totalitarian state in which almost every vestige of individual freedom has been obliterated. Big Brother watches over everybody with the help of sophisticated surveillance systems and thought police. Even the past is subsumed under the Party's total control of the present. Yesterday's newspapers are updated to conform with today's party line. Language has no power to convey any reality other than what the state propaganda machine prescribes. It has been stretched to the point of being able to make affirmations out of contradictions, like "war is peace" or "love is hate." This linguistic phenomenon is called "doublethink." The people have lost their memories and the ability to think for themselves. Under threat of liquidation they have become accustomed to adjusting their perspective to the latest official outlook.

There are, however, two persons who are covertly thinking their own thoughts and living their own lives. They possess a subversive piece of knowledge. This knowledge makes them enemies of the state, and ultimately they meet the fate of all who step out of line. But there is, nonetheless, something noble about their resistance, even though their spirits are eventually broken and the story ends in unremitting darkness.

What is this subversive piece of knowledge? It is not a mathematical formula that might enable them to crack the system or devise an alternative one. Nor is it some damaging information about the ruling party. It is neither practical advice nor a word of wisdom. It is nothing more than a scrap of a child's nursery rhyme: "Oranges and lemons say the bells of St. Clements. . . ."

How could this little rhyme threaten the power of the totalitarian state? By proffering a greater power—the power of metaphor to evoke another world. This nursery rhyme does not fit the current picture. It is from outside Big Brother's domain, and therefore beyond Big Brother's control. As such it contains within it the seed of revolution. The power of metaphor cannot guarantee the success of the revolution, as the book poignantly shows. But it does exhibit that infection that the human spirit is never without as long as it remains human and wills to be free.

When we come to talk of metaphor, then, we are speaking of something that comes close to what it is to be human. It is the power to name: This is that. In primitive societies this power to name carries a magical connotation. Words have power to effect what they say, as we see in the biblical account of creation, in which the world is created by God's word. That the power to name is given to Adam reveals a partnership between creature and Creator in making the world. The world is unfinished without human participation in naming. The importance of this naming for humanity has been emphasized by feminist theologians. That Eve is excluded from the naming process is a serious deficiency in the biblical story. For women to realize fully their humanity they must also participate in naming the world.

In the history of language the primitive magical sense of metaphor gradually gave way to conceptual and descriptive uses of language. Northrop Frye calls these subsequent phases of language metonymic and demotic. Whereas metaphors identify word and thing—"This is that"—metonymic language says, "This is *put for* that."[2] It is the language of explanation in continuous prose. The meaning of symbol and metaphor is interpreted allegorically into conceptual language. The world is divided into inner and outer, subject and object, transcendent and immanent, supernatural and natural, and continuity between the two spheres is maintained by analogy. The deductive mode of reasoning prevails. The standard of truth is coherence within reality. Authority comes from above.

The descriptive use of language depends on human powers of observation. Language corresponds with the reality being described. There is still the dualism of subject and object, but the analogy between the two no longer pertains. Objectivity has become the measure of what is true. The language of observation pertains only to relations within nature and is therefore unable to express transcendence. The inductive mode of reasoning prevails. The language is called demotic (of the people) because authority resides with the individual who has the power to observe.

Although these phases of language can be loosely associated with periods of history—ancient, medieval, and modern—they exist, to some degree, in every age. Because the concern is with metaphor, I shall restrict my observations to that. In the metonymic phase, as already stated, metaphor gives way to allegory. Metaphor no longer conveys its own meaning. It is no more than a way of illustrating a conceptual truth. As such, images and metaphors are used in poetry in a figurative way, but the meaning of the poem can be interpreted without the use of figurative language. Liturgy becomes an elaborate allegory that illustrates dogmatic truths. In the descriptive phase metaphor is avoided if possible because it interferes with a straightforward delineation of the facts. Both poetry and liturgy suffer, being relegated to the subjective sphere of reality having to do only with private thoughts and feelings. Metaphor is lost as a language that can express the whole of reality.

I have traced the gradual breakdown of the relationship between religion and philosophy with the attendant loss of transcendence. I can now identify more closely this loss of transcendence with the loss of metaphor, first in allegory and finally in the language of objectivity. In this situation the language of worship is thought to express, at best, a residual relationship with part of reality acknowledged by only a few, or it gives way to silence. The recovery of transcendence depends on a recovery of metaphor as a means of expressing the whole of reality. This recovery of metaphor will involve discovering once again the power of metaphor to name the world and thereby make of the world a human place to be.

Recent studies of language affirm that a recovery of metaphor is under way in all disciplines of thought after a long period of confinement within conceptual and descriptive language only. Sallie McFague, in her book *Metaphorical Theology*,[3] provides an excellent account of the recovery of metaphor not only in theology, but also in the scientific disciplines that were hitherto thought to be most objective and therefore devoid of metaphor. Indeed, as McFague shows, scientific uses of models as a way of approaching reality are pointing the way to a recovery of metaphor in the whole of language. Scientists no longer believe that they can approach reality purely objectively. The observer, as well as the thing being observed, has to be included in their calculations. Indeed, in the relationship between subject and object, the object is always at the disposal of the subject, and so, paradoxically, as the philosopher Martin Heidegger has noted, pure objectivity is subjectivity. To become conscious of the effect of the observer on the thing observed is to become more sensitive to otherness. It is toward this end that models serve a purpose.

Models and metaphors are means of naming reality that remains always other and, therefore, beyond our immediate comprehension. They bespeak the status of a participant rather than that of an observer. The participant does not have reality at her or his disposal. The relationship is not a direct one. Reality is mediated to us by means of metaphor. This is no longer metaphor in the primitive magical sense, which posited a direct relationship of identity between word and thing. To the "this is that" of primitive metaphor is added the indirection of "this is not that" so that no positive identification can be made.[4] The naming of metaphor does not have the power of bringing that which is named into being. Its power is that of making what is absent present or bringing that which is hidden to light. The otherness of what is named always remains. The power of metaphor is not that of disposal, but rather the power of being in community. The philosopher Martin Buber depicted the relationship as one that allows the object also to be a subject—an I-Thou relationship as opposed to an I-It relationship. And according to Buber, "real life is meeting."[5]

Recalling the Bible's prohibition of graven images one can now interpret the injunction in the light of modern understanding of metaphor. Then it was metaphor in the magical sense that was being prohibited as inadequate to express the relationship between God and the world of nature and history. God could not be identified with any part of creation and thus could not be directly apprehended, as could the gods of the other religions. Human beings do not have the power to name *YHWH*, who is known only as "I am that I am," or as, in another more dynamic translation, "I will be what I will be." And yet the Hebrews used many images and metaphors for God. God is a rock, a spring of water, a tree, a hen sheltering her young under her wing, and more. The multiplicity of images for God expresses the inadequacy of any single image to comprehend who God is.[6] This multiplicity exhibits the indirection of modern metaphor rather than the identification of the primitive metaphor—the *is not* as well as the *is*. Feminist theologians have rightly noted that absolutizing one metaphor, such as "father" for God, is a form of idolatry that the Bible itself prohibits.[7]

The Bible does not proscribe the use of a multiplicity of symbols and metaphors in its own language about God. There should be no compunction, therefore, about a rich use of metaphor, both verbal and visual, in liturgy. The parables of Jesus are metaphors. They are even more indirect, as McFague notes, than Old Testament language about God because they focus, not on the divine nature itself, but on the quality of the divine-human relationship called the kingdom or rule of God.[8] It is possible also to see Jesus' own life as a parable or metaphor of the rule of God, expressing both the *is* and the *is not* of God's presence in the world. The New Testament's metaphorical transference of ritual language from the sacred realm to include the whole of life introduces the metaphorical note of *is* and *is not* into Christian ritual. The ritual has no reality apart from the life of the Christian in the ordinary world beyond ritual.

This examination of metaphor enables us to consider the hermeneutical question: "What happens in worship?" The question itself posits a dynamic, rather than a static or passive, view of worship. Worship as metaphor *effects* something. It does not merely reflect or signify. It is a "word-event" and "sign-act."[9] With the power of its language to make what is absent present and to bring to light that which is hidden, it brings community into being—community between God and human beings and human beings with one another. Without the words and sign-acts of worship, people would be alone.

But how is this communion in worship to be understood? The

church has always understood its sacraments to be means of communion between God and humanity. The bread and wine of the Eucharist have been identified in Catholic theology as the "Real Presence" of God in Christ with the worshiper. This understanding derived from a theology of the Incarnation that affirmed God's presence in the person of Jesus and extended it, on the basis of Jesus' own words at the meal in the Upper Room: "This is my body." "This is my blood." Medieval theology interpreted the meaning of these statements in terms of the doctrine of transubstantiation, whereby the bread and wine were thought not only to symbolize Christ's body and blood, but actually to become so, by means of a miraculous transformation of the substance of the elements while the accidents or outer attributes remained the same.

Behind this doctrine was, as previously noted, a sacramental view of the universe that saw all things as participating in the reality of the divine by analogy *(analogia entis)*, and thus capable of becoming vehicles of divine presence. Here the emphasis was on continuity between the supernatural and the natural. In the sacraments of the church they become identical. The Reformers saw in this view of the identity of the divine and the human in the sacraments a danger of idolatry through the attribution to the symbols themselves of mysterious supernatural powers in their own right. Their protest can be seen as part of a wider movement, which we have seen in philosophy, that eventually led to the disintegration of the sacramental universe and loss of transcendence. The recovery of transcendence that is now under way is not a reinstating of the sacramental universe with its sense of continuity between human and divine. This is clearly lost for most people. What is more strongly sensed are the discontinuities in life, and the lack of identity between the world of nature and history and what can now be spoken of only as the Beyond. There is a connection with the transcendent, but it can only be pointed to, never grasped, within any facet of human experience.

Metaphors, with their "tensive, discontinuous and surprising nature,"[10] can be vehicles of transcendence in the modern age. Sacraments, understood as metaphors, will express both the *is* and the *is not* of our human experience of the Divine. Beside the sense of the presence of God will be an awareness of God's absence, the *Deus absconditus*, as well as the *Deus revelatus*. We have encountered this disjunction in Christian faith already in the *as though not* of Paul's understanding of the freedom of the Christian. It occurs also in the reversal of expectations that characterizes Jesus' parables of the kingdom. It is now most often understood with reference to the future that is promised by God—a future that is *not yet* and yet can be anticipated and celebrated in the present in the church's sacraments. This eschatological outlook is replacing the traditional substance categories of the sacramental universe in worship and in all our language about God.[11] The more static experience of being in God's presence in worship is replaced by an expectant and dynamic attitude of awaiting and experiencing God's coming. The sacraments as metaphor can express both the *is* and the *is not* of this coming. They have the metaphor's revolutionary capacity to evoke another world. The world they evoke is the one promised in the gospel and depicted in the Eucharist as a meal to which everyone is invited.

The ordinariness of this expectation, being a matter of ordinary food and drink, places it squarely within the realm of human history and its conflicting movements by which human beings benefit or are oppressed. History is the sphere of God's saving activity. The reality of the sacraments is not guaranteed by any supernatural working out of the divine intention in them apart from human agency, but in the actual participation of human beings in God's promise as a commitment toward the future of this world. Christians have to assess and become engaged in those movements in history that are most promising for the future. This engagement involves an element of subversion in relation to the present ruling powers. It is not peripheral to the authentic expression of liturgy, then, that many Christians are now engaged in movements for peace, for the rights of women and oppressed minorities, of concern for the natural environment, and for the liberation of the poor in the Third World countries. There have been more martyrs for the faith in the twentieth century than in any other period of church history. Is this not a confirmation of the connection between the vision of a better world glimpsed in worship and the struggle to attain that new world?

At this time in history this social and political commitment of Christian faith puts it on a path of convergence or collision with Marxism, which is also motivated by a revolutionary vision. Marx interpreted the dynamic of history in terms of class struggle—capitalist and worker, oppressor and the oppressed. Today the struggle that Marx identified continues within the affluent societies of the West, in which there are still disadvantaged people, and especially in Third World countries, in which oppressed populations are rising up against their oppressors. These people hear in Marxism a promise of hope. Many Christians among the poor and those who have heard in the gospel a call to join with the struggle of the poor have found in Marx a kindred spirit, and in Marxist analysis a way of understanding their situation and the revolution it calls for. Marx's call for justice on behalf of the oppressed puts him within the tradition of the Hebrew prophets. Marx's opposition to religion as giving a divine sanction to the existing situation, however, was not like the prophet's call for the reform of religion. Marx rejected religion and worship as standing in the way of revolution by fostering a false hope for salvation in another world beyond. He was speaking within the atheism of his day, which rejected the very idea of God and the supernatural. Marx, like his predecessor Feuerbach, also rejected the use of metaphor in language in favor of a direct apprehension of reality. There is to be observed a connection between this rejection of metaphor and the loss of transcendence.

We have now to look at the implications of the rejection of metaphor by Marx as we consider how Christians engage with Marxists in a common pursuit of social justice. Marx rejected worship and its use of metaphor. But does the worshiping community have to reject Marxism and its revolutionary zeal?

Contrary to Marx's view of religion and worship, I have sought to show the revolutionary impulse in worship and the empowerment it brings to human beings who are powerless in their own strength. This empowerment comes through participation in the power of the Creator God, who gives life to human beings by calling them into a new future anticipated in the Spirit. The words and sign-acts of worship are metaphors of participation in this future before it is fully realized. The future is experienced as hope. Can there be revolution without the power of the metaphor to evoke another world? Is there any empowerment without worship?

Marxism, in its original form, had its secular version of eschatology in the belief that the dialectic of history was moving toward a harmonious resolution of conflict in the classless society. The call to revolution was thus an invitation to enter into the movement of history. Those who did not enter were branded as "unhistorical" and hence expendable. But this Enlightenment article of faith has about the same persuasive power now as Adam Smith's opposite, but equivalent, free enterprise doctrine of the "invisible hand" that guides the conflicting demands of the marketplace toward economic equilibrium. The poor, in this case, because of their inability to participate in the marketplace, are the expendable ones. And on both sides there are still some true believers!

But more compelling to the poor, no doubt, has been Marx's raising of their consciousness to a recognition of their plight. The fuel for revolution is the indignation of the oppressed against the oppressor. And this fuel, once it is tapped, is never in short supply. Revolution, then, becomes a deadly serious business with no room for ordinary work or play or the simple joys that keep life human. Before the revolution has reached its goal it has forgotten how life is to be lived. Emma Goldman, in her autobiography, *Living My Life*, has put her finger on the problem: If I can't dance, I don't want to be part of the revolution. [12]

The revolution needs the dance. It cannot get along without the indirection of metaphor that may appear to be a distraction, but is that which prevents the revolution from becoming absolute. In the USSR we see a revolution that has absolutized a current state of affairs under the rule of a totalitarian regime. Intrinsic to the power of a totalitarian state is a rejection of metaphor, as we see in Orwell's *1984*. Among a people with a wonderfully rich heritage of art and liturgy, the Communist Party in Russia has suppressed the arts and religion wherever it can, although by no means entirely successfully. The state opposes dissident art in favor of official symbolism. This symbolism portrays the reality that conforms with the ideology of the state. But unlike the indirection of metaphor that allows diverse interpretations and awakens the imagination, there is something blatant and overpowering about the official symbolism, as seen in the representation of muscles and tractors in Socialist Realism, the official art of the Soviet Union, or the parade of military might on May Day, or the drive toward athletic supremacy that causes such consternation among its free-world competitors. Symbol has become spectacle. The weakness of metaphor is replaced by a display of sheer force. Nothing remains hidden. There is no possibility of a variety of interpretations or subtle nuances. The message is univocal.

Capitalist countries are not immune to this perversion of symbol into spectacle and reduction to the obvious. Children learn to read by following the adventures of Dick and Jane and Spot or their latest incarnations. The dominant art form is to be found in advertisements, half-time shows, and evangelical religious extravaganzas. The film *Dr. Strangelove* gives an as-yet-unsurpassed portrayal of the lunacy of the nuclear age's fascination with raw power expressed in the two most prevalent myths in American society—football and the Western cowboy. George C. Scott, the general, exults in the thought of "throwing the long bomb" and Slim Pickins, with cowboy hat in hand, whoops it up as he rides the bomb to obliteration.

The saving grace of American society, with its pressures toward unswerving conformity, is the freedom to create and view such films as this, criticizing the tendencies that would take away the freedoms. The American revolutionary founders understood the tendency in human nature to absolutize when they created a government with built-in checks and balances, and allowed an expansive society to emerge where there is room for dissent. This liberal philosophy, however, may not be so much a philosophy as a reflection of spacious times, when there is plenty of room to expand. When times get tight, as in recent years, the liberal attitude tends to disappear and be replaced by an attitude of constraint that can become violent. The first to experience the violence are the people on the periphery of American society, including minorities at home, and, outside its borders, neighboring countries such as Chile, Nicaragua, or even Canada, where the

option of toeing the line seems no less confining than what is offered in countries like Poland and Afghanistan within the Soviet sphere of influence.

It is a known fact that language suffers in the hands of a totalitarian regime. First to disappear is the indirection of metaphor in favor of the lie that is presented as univocal speech. Where worship is allowed, it too suffers by being absorbed by the accepted myths of civil religion. Some of these symptoms can be seen in Western society. Worship as praise gets misdirected as a sanction for current conditions rather than pointing to a God who transcends the principalities and powers. It is a question worth pondering, then, whether, at this time in the history of Western society, worship is too easy because it has lost the metaphors that surprise and disturb the rhythm of the prevailing situation. Where is to be heard the beat of a different drummer, to use Thoreau's phrase? Has our worship become like the worship that Paul found in Corinth (1 Corinthians 11), where the metaphors of a communion of God's love coexisted with a community characterized by a lack of caring? One could think that such empty metaphors simply do not matter. But Paul takes a more serious view of their effect. He says to the Corinthians: "You are eating and drinking judgment on yourselves." Perhaps this residual efficacy of the metaphors in judging is reason enough not to follow Juan Segundo's counsel in *The Sacraments Today*, in which he suggests a moratorium on the sacraments until they can once again express an authentic relationship between the sacred and the secular.[13] Authentic worship, then, may be no easier in a democratic society, where it is allowed, than in those societies that actively suppress it.

But if we are to continue to worship, how can we do so authentically? This is much more, as Segundo has noted, than a problem of "correcting defects in the liturgy."[14] It will involve, no doubt, seeking to bring our lives into line with our liturgy. But for this we need the empowerment that the liturgy provides, that we may live by the freedom of the gospel and not simply under the law. What is called for first is an openness to the "tensive, discontinuous and surprising nature" of the metaphors of the gospel we experience in worship. It is openness to God as the One who creates and makes new and invites us, as renewed creatures, to participate in making the world. We can call this a grateful awareness of the givenness of life, or an expectant attitude toward a future that is open but full of promise. Before all else this worship will be an act of praise—an action that has no other purpose than to glorify the Giver of life, and is, therefore, purposeless as regards our human plans and programs. This sheer purposelessness of worship sets it apart from all human purposes. It is the ultimate metaphor of discontinuity. This purposelessness is not apathy or lack of caring. Christians share with Marxists the revolutionary spirit. But their greatest contribution to the revolution, beyond their revolutionary zeal, is in preventing it from becoming absolute. Christians can never be safe revolutionaries who can be counted on to subordinate every value to the revolutionary goal. The metaphors of worship do not allow it. Worship does allow, indeed it enables, people to dance even in the most trying circumstances of life. It is the dance of freedom, without which life is not human.

Viewed from the outside, the worship of Christians may be seen as nothing more than an odd quirk or even a piece of whimsy left over from another age—a church steeple pointing skyward among a forest of taller structures designed to reflect the power and affluence of their corporate builders, or a child's nursery rhyme about church bells ringing: "Oranges and lemons say the bells of St. Clements. . . ." To passersby, who are intent on going somewhere, it may be an invitation to stop and dance—a momentary diversion that brightens the day and lightens the step.

The worshipers themselves may not fully comprehend what they are doing. When they are few in number they may be tempted to despair by the sheer weakness and futility of what they are doing. And yet they may simply let themselves pause to rejoice in their Maker and Partner in creation, perhaps becoming aware that this is a distinctive action that they do, beyond the good work they share with others of good will—setting up a sign of faith in a world that has forgotten or never known the One to whom it owes its being and on whom its future depends. In doing this they are the church acting vicariously for the world with their Savior who died on a cross for the sake of all. The authenticity of the church's praise is in its willingness to offer up its life in the world, letting its life correspond with its liturgy. This sacrifice of a life offered up in praise and thanksgiving, of which the cross is a perpetual sign, is, as Paul said, the weakness and foolishness that is the wisdom and power of God.

I am able now, instead of speaking of praise and empowerment, to say that praise *is* empowerment, in the strange sense of indirection I have noted in the *is* and *is not* of metaphor. Praise is empowerment because it does not intend to be. It is the action of a life offered up rather than that of a life at one's own disposal. Such a life, in its weakness and vulnerability, as seen in the cross and resurrection of Jesus Christ, is invincible.

I mentioned earlier how closely metaphor is bound up with human nature. Where metaphor is suppressed, human life itself is threatened. It has been said of artists that they are like the rabbits that used to be carried in submarines. When the air was becoming unfit to support life, the rabbits would be the first to succumb, thereby warning the human inhabitants of the impending danger to their lives while there was still time for remedial action. Artists in a society that devalues human life are usually among the first to be banished or to die. Let it be said of the worship of the church, too, that its offering of praise is a test of the humanity of the society rather than, as Marx found, the upholder of the conditions that diminish human life.

PART THREE

What Can Happen
in Worship

8

Sunday Morning: Gathering and Sending Forth

What happens on Sunday morning? My study of liturgy as praise and empowerment comes down to this question concerning the time when Christians gather for worship. It is a question that takes one beyond ritual to the whole of life. Consequently the more basic question "What elements in human experience give rise to worship?" and a subsequent question, "What is the outcome of worship in daily life?" become relevant.

With regard to its origins and outcome we have traced the impulse for worship from its origin in the most basic aspects of human life—the experience of givenness—an experience that points backward to the beginning of life in a vision of creation, and forward to the end and culmination of life in an apocalyptic vision. Between this beginning and end and as an outcome of their worship Christians live out their lives in the world as an expression of the freedom that is celebrated and empowered in worship. Sunday worship can be justly regarded as the gathering place for everything Christians do and are affected by.

But sometimes worship, as a response to the givenness of life, has related only to that part of human experience that can be identified as passivity. Such worship provides, or seeks, a refuge from the demands of historical and natural existence in the service of a higher being or by acquiescing in the natural or supernatural forces that are perceived to determine human existence. Such worship can be theologically categorized as being under the law. Law is the designation for the basic order and structure that governs the whole of existence. In nature it can be identified with the passage of time in hours and seasons and with the limits of a given space. In history it finds expression in institutions and codified laws. These are the determining factors for life. Worship within the legal sphere is characterized as passivity because there is no movement beyond what the law can compel or enforce. There is no empowerment. In practice such worship has usually reflected and helped to perpetuate the master-slave relationship that runs through the whole of history.

Worship, as it emerged among the ancient Hebrews and is continued by Christians, breaks with the passivity by embracing also the activity of human beings. The worshipers experience themselves as creatures in a world that God has made and, at the same time, as called to participate as co-creators in God's plan for the future of the world. My study of worship in the New Testament found that the movement of worship was grounded in freedom rather than in law. The participant in Christian worship celebrates the freedom of the gospel in an act of praise and is empowered to live that freedom in the world. The givenness of life, as understood within the category of gospel, includes both the origin of life in God's gracious actions in the past and openness to the new as the future God has in store for the world. Givenness, therefore, no longer means passivity in relation to that which is. It means openness to that which is to come, to the call of the future. This openness means being willing to engage in that call.

This worship with its active engagement in time—with the events that make up human history—can be understood as a movement in time. Worship is timely, not static or timeless. It has a beginning and an outcome in time, being open to and effecting growth, development, and change. But it is not determined by time. That which transcends time in this worship, however, exists not in a separate permanent sphere of the sacred or eternal, but within time as its opening to the beyond. Worship expresses the mystery of the givenness of time in a world in which the law of time is experienced as time inevitably passing away. To receive the gift of time is to experience grace over against the law of the passage of time; it is to have free time—a time within which human beings have the freedom for that quality of life known as agape (love). Bonhoeffer has called this life an "existence for others." It is, as he said, a participation in transcendence understood as worldliness. Christian worship participates in transcendence, not apart from, but in the midst of worldly living. It does so by means of metaphors that express both the connection and the disjunction of this world with the beyond.

The choice of Sunday by Christians as a day of worship has this character of metaphor. The early Christians thought of Sunday as both the first day of the week and the eighth day—an eschatological day, both inside and outside of time, that marks the beginning of the reign of God. In contrast to the Jewish sabbath on Saturday, Sunday is not simply a hallowed day of rest at the end of the week's labor. Nor is it a day like other days for fulfilling the demands of daily work. Sunday can best be understood as free time, and as such a time of new beginnings. Sunday, the first day of the week, as Justin said in the second century, is the day when God began to create the universe and our Savior Jesus Christ rose from the dead. Sunday, the eighth day, the first day of the New Age, marks the future reign of God that is already in the present breaking into time. In this strange disjunction of past and future, first day and last day, Christians worship on Sunday in an action by which the church is brought into existence and is sustained in its life and mission.

What happens on Sunday morning? The question itself points to the dynamic nature of worship as liturgy—as a work of the people. Liturgy can be conceived of as a movement constituting outward words and sign-acts and a corresponding movement in the minds and hearts of the people who participate. Theological treatments of worship have customarily thought of worship more in terms of order or structure than in terms of movement. The value of discoveries pertaining to shape and order for the modern renewal of liturgy cannot be denied. Gregory Dix's *The Shape of the Liturgy*[1] is a most noted example of such a study. But the concept of order, as applied to liturgy, can betray too static a view of what happens in worship. Sometimes preoccupation with order has led to a juridical approach that gives too much value to uniformity as opposed to freedom in worship. Even those so-called free churches, which have opposed uniformity in favor of worship guided by directories or entirely free worship, have usually not escaped the rigidity of an order that has no life in it. One does not arrive at a vital expression of worship by filling in the blanks in an order of service anymore than by adhering assiduously to the letter (in this case a prescribed liturgy). Those who seek sheer spontaneity often fall into a pattern that is as confining as, or even more confining than, unvarying directories and formulated liturgies. Nor does one come to an understanding of what happens in worship simply by dissecting or analyzing it. Worship is better understood as a body that has life and movement. As a body it has a form or shape that varies according to its movement and direction while retaining its basic identity. Knowing it, as one knows a living being, albeit, in the case of worship, as a corporate rather than as an individual being, is always a matter of relationship, of following its movements.

Recent studies in liturgical theology have used a method of reasoning from the "outward and visible forms by which Christians worship,"[2] which implies this relationship of following between liturgy and theology. Modern study of the nature of language and symbol in phenomenology and hermeneutics has provided a conceptual basis for thinking of worship in relational and dynamic rather than in static terms. The awareness of human beings as embodied creatures whose "bodies speak a language of gesture"[3] has broken down the division between outer and inner, visible and invisible, form and content, that has so bedeviled worship in the past. Language is rooted in gesture. Gestures are not subsequent to thoughts and feelings. They *enact* thoughts and feelings. An embrace, for example, is not "a weak translation" of a prior feeling of affection; it is a way of being affectionate. Words and symbols, like gestures, *effect* something; they do not merely signify something prior.[4] It is possible, then, to speak of word-events and sign-acts as a way of capturing the dynamic nature of language that includes both the movement of the outward sounds and sights and the corresponding movements in the minds and hearts of the people who participate. It is not hard to see why this way of thinking is giving rise to new ways of understanding both word and sacraments in liturgy, thereby opening avenues for ecumenical convergence.

Recognizing the weakness in "formalistic" approaches to liturgy, the Orthodox theologian Alexander Schmemann has acknowledged the importance of what is happening in the minds and hearts of the people as well as in the "Ordo" of worship. He takes account of this inner movement with his concept of "liturgical piety." Liturgical piety "is the psychological acceptance of the cult, its experience within the religious mind, its refraction within the consciousness of the believer."[5] What is happening in liturgy, according to Schmemann, cannot be fully understood without consideration of the liturgical piety. Indeed liturgical piety featured largely in the changes that took place especially after Constantine. These changes, however, are not regarded as fundamental or revolutionary by Schmemann.[6] Ordo remains as the defining characteristic, even though worship, as he acknowledges, had changed after Constantine, from being a celebration of freedom to a legalistic cult. Schmemann cannot acknowledge this change as theologically fundamental because he regards the Ordo, rather than liturgical piety, as the basis for liturgical theology. Liturgical piety is given no more than psychological status.

Here, on the contrary, I am arguing that liturgical theology, rooted in metaphor, takes account of both the outer and the inner movements—of both the Ordo and the liturgical piety. It is of the nature of metaphors to evoke in people's minds and hearts that to which they point because they are relational and dynamic, enabling participation. If they do not do so, they are ineffectual as metaphor and, therefore, to be discounted for liturgy in favor of more suitable ones. One, for example, has to question the adequacy of the tray of little glasses that serves many Protestant churches as a substitute for the cup. As a metaphor the separate glasses do not express the unity that is to be implied in the action of communion.

There has been in the discipline of homiletics a parallel development to the one that has discerned the dynamic nature of language and symbol in liturgy. The implications of this language study for homiletics has virtually brought about its rebirth as a theological discipline. A few years ago preaching was usually taught by an outstanding preacher who offered a few how-to lectures accompanied by exercises on making sermon outlines. The sermon outlines, which were subsequently to be filled in, particularly revealed a static conception of the sermon, even if one did not precisely adhere to the recommended introduction, three points, and a poem! Grady Davis, in his 1956 book *Design for Preaching*,[7] was one of the first to offer a more dynamic approach, with his emphasis on starting with an idea that can grow. What distinguishes this "idea" from a mere theme or topic is that it has a tension within it that evokes something in the minds and hearts of the hearers that calls for exploration or resolution. The "Spirit of Thanksgiving," for example, is a topic or theme that gives no indication as to where the sermon might go. In contrast, a sermon on Jesus' story of the thankful Pharisee and the remorseful tax collector who went into the temple to pray titled "The Temptation of Thanksgiving" contains an idea that builds a tension and thereby evokes an immediate response in the hearer. Davis' homiletical theory was taking account not only of how a sermon is constructed, but also of what is happening in the hearer and how the sermon moves with the hearer and empowers the hearer to new awareness and action. The sermon, therefore, in Reuel Howe's words, is dialogical rather than monological.[8] Subsequent homileticians have refined this approach with their studies of the dynamic nature of language and metaphor. Recent studies have been ascribing to the sermon the movement of a narrative. Few writers in homiletics, moreover, would regard the sermon apart from its place within the total movement of the liturgy and, therefore, affected by what comes before and after. I shall be looking at the sermon or the homily in the context of the liturgy in chapter 9. I now turn to look more closely at the movement of the liturgy.

Paul Hoon has said that "the *esse*—the being—of the church is apostolic or missionary, so the *esse* of worship must embody apostolicity."[9] This statement conforms with what we learned of worship in the New Testament as transferring the cultic language into language about everyday life. Beside this must be set the description of the church and its worship from earliest times as gathering or assembly. This meaning is exemplified in such early designations for worship as *ecclesia* (assembly) and *synaxis* or *synagogue* (meeting). The dynamic of worship can be found in the tension of this movement of gathering and sending forth. This movement has been compared with the systolic and diastolic movement of the heart, which draws the life-giving blood into itself and sends it forth throughout the body. In the liturgy this movement of gathering and sending forth is made explicit in the opening and closing portions of the order.

Within the eucharistic order of worship there are two meeting places: under the Word and around the Table. These two main sections, the Service of the Word and the Service of the Table, follow immediately on the brief introductory or Gathering Section and precede the concluding section in which the people are sent forth. The Service of the Word has its origin in the worship of the Jewish synagogue. The Service of the Table harkens back to the meal in the Upper Room before the crucifixion, but also to the many meals Jesus shared during his ministry with his followers and friends, including tax collectors and sinners, and after his resurrection, as at Emmaus (Luke 24:13–35) and in Galilee (John 21:4–14). Furthermore, Jesus' own vision of the coming kingdom was depicted in parables as a great feast (Matthew 22:1–14, Luke 14:15–24) and actualized during his ministry in the miraculous feeding of the five thousand. These two services that first existed separately on Saturday and Sunday were unified as early as the middle of the second century, as we can see from Justin's account of worship on Sunday or "the Lord's Day" in Rome about A.D. 150.

Each of these meeting places in the unified service—under the Word and around the Table—includes an outward direction as well as a gathering. The Service of the Word includes both proclamation of the Word and the people's response. The Word is proclaimed in the readings of scripture that are a thankful rehearsing or telling of the story of faith. The sermon continues the proclamation by bringing the scriptural word and the lives of the people together in a word for today. As such the sermon includes both proclamation of the Word and the people's response. The people see their own lives evoked by story and metaphor in the sermon and are enabled in the light of the gospel to gain a fresh insight into and commitment for living in the freedom of faith. After the sermon the prayers of the people are offered by the people as they see their lives anew in the light of the preached word. This prayer, with its turning outward in intercession, is the beginning of the people's exercise of pastoral care and mission in the world.

Whereas in the Service of the Word the movement is first from God to us before our response, the movement of the Service of the Table begins with us, in our self-offering, in the presentation of gifts, and culminates in an act of communion wherein we receive the gifts back again transformed into the Body of Christ. Eating and drinking together we are united with one another and with God in preparation for worldly living as members of Christ's Body. The table fellowship, as a "heavenly feast," includes an eschatological vision of the future God has in store for the whole world. It is this vision that nourishes and empowers the Christian people for their mission in the world.

I shall deal in more detail with the movement of the Service of the Word and the Service of the Table in subsequent chapters. Here it is sufficient to say that in each of these meeting places a miracle of transformation takes place as the people and the world with its concerns are gathered in God's presence. The sermon or homily gives expression to our human situation in the transforming light of the gospel. The eucharistic meal receives its matter from the gifts that the people present as the substance of their own lives. At these meeting points both worshipers and world are transformed by God's gracious presence. This miracle has variously been talked about in terms of transubstantiation, conversion or sanctification, and, more recently, eschatology.

The eschatological character of Christian worship arises out of the expectation that God will actually be met in the worship gathering and that God's presence grants a new future. The missionary or apostolic character of worship comes as a call into this future that is being opened in word and sacrament. The sign of this coming future is the dawning presence of the Spirit (epiclesis). Its direction has already been revealed in the history of Israel, culminating in the life and ministry, crucifixion and resurrection of Jesus. This history continues in the church through the living presence of the risen Lord (anamnesis). The gathering and mission of the church that exist in the tension between anamnesis and epiclesis, between remembering and hoping, are open realities that extend into all times and places.

It follows from this openness that there are at least two distinguishing marks of Christian praise: expectancy and inclusivity.

Expectancy and inclusivity can be readily discerned in terms of the congregation's openness to new possibilities and to all sorts and conditions of people in their midst. The opposite of these marks is complacency and exclusivity. The former occurs when praise of God becomes no more than a satisfied acquiescing in the status quo with no anticipation of a new action of God. The latter is evident when some voices or faces are absent from the gathering or leadership of the assembly, be they children, elderly, the poor, the disabled, women, or other of the disregarded. The ancient Hebrews were cognizant of both these marks of true worship in their concern to welcome the stranger. In closing the door on the stranger, they believed, they could be denying God entry into their midst. Christians have the same desire to exclude no one so as not to give a false picture of the Body of Christ in their worship.

This leads us now to take a close look at who takes part in the movement of gathering and sending forth that characterizes Christian worship. Clearly the simple answer is that people do. People worshiping, more than the buildings in which they worship, are the most visible sign of the church. The designation "liturgy" or "people's work" for worship underlines this ordinary fact of Christian worship. Worship exists at the level of ordinary human interaction. But it goes beyond the mundane level too. It transcends the ordinary but in a strange paradoxical way. Our ordinary life is not left behind as if we were entering some extraordinary realm—a timeless, sacred sphere cut off from secular life. Rather, we encounter in worship the extraordinary in the ordinary. A meeting of earth and heaven takes place. In worship we acknowledge a reality that goes far beyond the limited, "one-dimensional" sphere within which we are normally wont to live our lives.

Sometimes the perception of children in these matters is clearer than that of adults—another good reason children should be included in worship! We may recall Wordsworth's memory of the "celestial light" perceived in childhood that fades into "the light of common day." My wife, Nancy, and I, with our three-year-old son, Tommy, participated one summer in the worship of a large Gothic-style metropolitan church. There was not a full choir that day, but an anthem was sung by a quartet of the leading soloists. As they came out in their white robes to the center of the chancel to sing, my son leaned over to his mother and in his best Upper Ottawa valley dialect whispered: "Mummy, are them angels?" Now as adults (and knowing choirs as we do) we would never make that mistake in identification. But was there not some truth in this childlike perception of things—in the sense of wonder, the awareness of the "numinous," the ability to see the sacred in the ordinary?

Worship requires us to do precisely that! And so we can speak not only of ourselves gathered together—as if we were attending a meeting of the local service club—but also of a communion of saints—a community of faith that spans all ages and places. We can speak of heavenly beings. The psalms speak of stars that sing in praise of God—of angels and archangels. When we sing we join a heavenly host. Finally, and indeed before all else, we can speak of encountering God in worship. "God," says Paul Hoon, "is the first reality in worship, not [human beings]."[10]

What I have been describing is not the way we usually look at ourselves and what we do. Worship invites us to adopt a different attitude to ourselves and to the world in which we live, one that includes "wonder, love, and praise." In worship we no longer regard one another, as Paul says, "from a human point of view [2 Cor. 5:16]." This expanded reality governs everything that can be said about who takes part in worship or what they do. Worship uses metaphors and sign-acts to convey the strange sense of "indirection," "is and is not," that reveals worship's connection with the beyond. The worshiper needs to be sensitive to how symbols work in order to participate fully. A presider, for example, can give a complete misdirection to the service by beginning it with a friendly "Hello!" This greeting fails to take account of God's presence and puts the focus on the personality of the presider. Clericalism, in which clergy dominate by their presence, can happen in informal ways as well as in formal liturgies.

The metaphors and sign-acts of worship are, as previously seen, a way for people to be present to one another and to God. Word and sacraments are means chosen by God to be present with people. God is "embodied" in the sacraments. As Robert Jenson has said, "God's presence must grant an object."[11] In this respect Christianity differs from religions that seek to transcend the body.

116

Christian faith is through and through sacramental. The sacraments are God's loving gestures reaching out to touch, to heal, and to beckon God's people. It is this renewed understanding of worship as embodiment that leads Christians to seek or recover new forms of worship that address and express the whole person—including all the senses and all people's gifts. This is opening up vast areas for variety in worship using all the arts, including music, drama, dance, the spoken word, visual arts, and architecture. With this variety greater opportunity is given for showing and honoring the wealth of gifts that people can bring to worship.

This gathering of many gifts—constituting many voices, many faces, many hands—enables the true nature of the church to be revealed in worship as bodying forth God's rule in the world. Now being rediscovered is the ministry of all the baptized. Christians are a "royal priesthood" (1 Peter:2–9). Their worship is an exercise of sovereign freedom. The recovery of this freedom has required overcoming the passivity of the laity that has been so prevalent in history up to the present. Their growing participation in the worship of the church can be regarded as another of the liberation movements of our time, raising their consciousness for greater action as people of faith in the world.

It is becoming customary to speak of the participation of the people in worship and outreach or mission as a variety of ministries, instead of confining the term to the ordained. Many new ministries are emerging, not because somebody ordered it, but because of changes in the church and world. These ministries are a response to the question "How can the church and individual Christians be faithful in worship and mission now?" What are some of these ministries? In the liturgy, parts are emerging for readers, servers, cantors, prayer leaders, music directors, ushers, diaconal ministers, or assistants, and presiders. The term presider designates not one who does everything, but the unifying role or presidency function in a community action in which many are taking part. There are also people's parts, such as acclamations, responses, unison prayers, psalms, hymns, processions, gestures, and communal silence. Finally, occasional ministries are rendered in the visual arts, drama, instrumental and vocal music, and witnessing by word of mouth, including testimonies and spontaneous utterance.

This plethora of possibilities for ministry, resembling the situation described by Paul in 1 Corinthians 14, raises, as it did for him, the question of order. The purpose behind the ordering of all ministries is that they serve the one ministry of Jesus Christ in the world as this is expressed in the faith community's worship and mission. This ordering, therefore, is always a matter of theology rather than of expediency or even of democracy. The church can be no "respecter of persons," dispensing patronage in choosing its leaders. Nor does it merely pose the question "Whose turn is it?" Ordering ministry is a matter of the spirit, discerning needs and gifts. It can be done authentically only in communal prayer and in the light of the gospel.

The task of discerning must be followed by appropriate means of preparation and authorization so that the minister can serve effectively and in a way that represents the community's will. Occasional ministries are given recognition in the community's acceptance of the particular gift—be it a work of art, or playing an instrument, or dancing on a given occasion. Ministries that have a continuity of function, such as presiding, diaconal ministry, and music direction, need formalization by means of a service of recognition, blessing, commissioning, or ordination. The traditional means of recognizing special ministry in ordination is with prayer and the laying on of hands. Could this action not be fruitfully extended to all forms of ministry that serve a continuous function in the church or on behalf of the church in the world? Such a procedure might help to break down the sharp line of division that has separated clergy from laity through most of church history. As Edward Schillebeeckx points out,[12] this distinction does not appear in the New Testament. At the same time, differences, such as in the function and range of responsibility and representation among the ministries, could be distinguished in the words of the ordination prayer and in who the ordaining body is. A reader or music director in a congregation, for example, neither has nor needs authorization to function beyond the particular congregation. The local congregation would, therefore, be the agent of ordination. But a presider or diaconal minister represents the larger church and, therefore, receives authorization from some representative of the wider church (i.e., bishop, presbytery, or conference). The decisive thing in the service for designating a particular ministry would not be entry into a separate order, but empowerment by the Spirit through prayer and the laying on of hands of the people for particular service in and on behalf of the community of faith. Without this empowerment no spiritual ministry is possible.

A ministry in the church receives its initial authorization and empowerment in a service of installation or ordination. For its continuing function it receives authentication in the weekly Sunday liturgy as the gathering place for everything Christians do and are affected by. Ministry receives its profile or is given recognition in the symbolic roles of the liturgy. At the same time liturgical ministries must have a connection with some nonliturgical function in the community. A reader ought to be selected not only on the basis of whose turn it is or even of who is gifted. The reader needs not only the ability to read, but also the recognition of the community as one who is steeped in the scriptures and is actively engaged in fostering the community's attention to the Word in Bible study and teaching or outreach. An appropriate analogy might be with the news readers on TV. Should they be just pretty faces and pleasant voices, or should they also be reporters? The analogy breaks down when the announcer rightly stops short of making the news. The scripture reader does not only read the news; he or she is part of the community that is called to make the news. This connection between liturgical and nonliturgical ministry is necessary to show the intrinsic connection between worship and mission. The role of the presider in liturgy is unthinkable apart from an exercise of pastoral care. Likewise, a diaconal minister's leading of the Prayers of the People needs the connection with the outreach of the congregation as expressed in the concerns of that prayer. Where this connection is lost no effective ministry takes place.

I have thus far been speaking of ordering and authenticating the variety of ministries of the church. Because this variety of ministries presupposes the participation of the whole community of faith, both individually and corporately, the question of ordering gets extended into the whole matter of educating and organizing. Here we are speaking of the preparation and conduct of worship as a corporate responsibility rather than as one that is left to the clergy. Various possibilities are emerging in many congregations, including Bible study groups that are engaged with the preacher in the preparation of the sermon, youth and adult education based on the lectionary readings, groups responsible for pastoral care and outreach who have special responsibility for the Prayers of the People in the liturgy, weekly planning groups, and worship committees. Time during the week as well as immediately before the service can be given to rehearsing unfamiliar parts of the service and training readers, choirs, and congregations.

Many books on worship are available that are helpful for facilitating the people's involvement in the liturgy. Furthermore, rubrics that at one time presupposed only the action of the clergy are now being rewritten with the people's participation in mind. The aim of all these activities is the public worship of God as a corporate act of praise in which people are empowered both to celebrate and to live the freedom of the gospel in the world. Such an approach requires a major reordering of priorities on the part of both clergy and congregations if worship as praise and empowerment is to become an actuality rather than merely existing in theory. Liturgy as the praxis of faith and as the embodiment of the church demands such a commitment.

We have yet to see the full implications of this view of liturgy in the churches. In practice it would mean no less than redefining the catholicity of the church. In current denominational structuring of the churches the visible embodiment and the identity of the churches are seen, as in Roman Catholicism, in the hierarchical structure, and in the membership rolls of representative and governing bodies of Protestant churches. These structures probably have more to do with the way secular institutions have evolved in the West than with the reality of the church as the Body of Christ. If the liturgy, with its continuation in the church's ministry of outreach, were to become the sign of the corporate reality of the church, it could be expected that denominations would become less important to the expression of people's faith and loyalties. People would begin, in other words, to vote with their feet, according to where they found a genuine expression of the church's life and commitment in liturgy and mission.

This movement would constitute a serious threat to existing denominational structures (the financial implications alone are truly daunting!), but it would not be comparable to sectarian movements of the past that divided churches into new denominations. Rather, it would be a relocation of the focus of catholicity from the governing structures of the churches to the visible embodiment of the church in the liturgy. Such a relocation would no doubt be accompanied by new and as yet unforeseen institutional arrangements. It could also be an ecumenical breakthrough toward a new manifestation of the unity and historical continuity of the churches, joined together in praise of God and in service of God in the world. There is cause to believe that this new expression of ecumenicity is already happening among the churches after the decline of the earlier ecumenical movement, which had its focus in organizational reunion. As is perhaps to be expected, movements toward actual intercommunion among Christians of different denominations are being resisted by the hierarchical authorities of some churches. Nevertheless the current ecumenical convergence in worship is surely one of the most hopeful and indeed epochal events in the history of the church.

9

Service of the Word:
Proclamation and Response

Speaking of one of the focal points of the Sunday liturgy as a meeting under the Word gives a clear indication of the priority of God's Word over human life that is exhibited in the liturgy. It is not our human word, however eloquent or wise, that takes precedence in worship, but God's Word, which is acknowledged as a creating, judging, and redeeming word for human beings. We recognize the scriptures of the Old and New Testaments, not as identical with God's Word, but as a faithful witness to that Word insofar as they point to the events of God's covenant dealings with Israel and God's redeeming presence with us in Jesus Christ. The story as told in the scriptures, therefore, is given precedence in liturgy in the action of reading and hearing the scriptures. The worshiping community gathers under the Word each week to hear and to have its eyes opened to God's truth for human life. Jews and Christians take seriously the words of the psalmist in praise of the scriptures: "Thy word is a lamp to my feet and a light to my path [Ps. 119:105]."

The scriptures have this kind of authority for Christian faith—not that we *have* to believe in order to hear, but that we *can* believe because we have heard. This kind of authority is consistent with freedom because it achieves its effect by empowerment rather than by constraint. The German word for authority, *Vollmacht* (full power), perhaps better than our English word, designates the kind of authority of God's Word that empowers human freedom. Christians do not need to apologize for or seek to evade, therefore, the authority of God's Word in worship in favor of a freedom that in the post-Enlightenment era is perceived only as freedom from authority. We begin our worship, then, expecting something salutary from God's Word and, in a brief gathering section, prepare ourselves for hearing it.

The proclamation of the Word begins with the reading of scripture. Each reading may be preceded by a brief introduction that provides the setting or context of the passage in the scriptures, and be followed by a silent time for meditation and/or psalm, canticle, hymn or anthem. Here the freedom of the text must be guarded that it may simply be heard in its own right. The reader must read as one who hears rather than as one who has the Word at his or her disposal. This is not a time for memory work or the dramatic art of an actor, as if the Word were not coming out of a book. Nor should the introduction begin to tell the listeners what they should hear, as a kind of preacher's prelude to the sermon. For similar reasons a good translation is preferable to a paraphrase for use in liturgy.

The connection between the scripture readings and the sermon or homily should be clearly evident—affirmed both in time and in space—with the latter following immediately on the former and from the same place in the worship assembly. The use of both a pulpit and a lectern is a detriment to the unity of these actions. The sermon continues the proclamation of the Word with the intention of furthering its movement into the people's lives in a word for today. This is the primary movement of the sermon— from the text to our situation. There is another movement within the sermon—from our situation to the text. The sermon that contains both these movements is both proclamation and response. Already in the sermon the people's lives are brought to expression beside the text so that the scriptural word and our word may intersect. Out of this meeting under the Word comes new light for our situation that enables us to see ourselves and the world with the eyes of faith.

Following closely on the sermon comes the response of the people, which may take a variety of forms, including silent and/or individual reflections on the Word, a creed or hymn, baptism, reaffirmations of faith, announcements of congregational life and work, and the gathering of concerns for the Prayers of the People.

The Prayers of the People conclude the Service of the Word. Prayers are offered by the people as they see their lives anew in the light of the preached word. In this prayer the people can begin to exercise in prayer their renewed commitment to being God's people in the world, serving God's reign of justice and love. The movement of the Service of the Word readies the people for being reconciled with one another in the exchange of peace and for presenting their gifts at the altar table in the Service of the Table that follows.

The movements, I have briefly described, of the Service of the Word within the whole liturgy and of the sermon within the Service of the Word now need further elaboration. The movement of the liturgy reflects and focuses and enables a larger movement that happens in the life of the faith community in the world. What happens, then, in the Service of the Word can be fully understood only by looking at how the Word functions in the life of the community. The hearing of scripture takes place not only by liturgical reading, but also by interpreting the texts in relation to our present-day experience. The liturgy needs to be accompanied by Bible study, education, and acts of service.

Historical, critical, and literary study of the Bible has contributed immensely to the church's understanding of the scriptures. The need for interpretation arises out of the historical distance between the time of the writing of the scriptures and our own time. The Bible originally addressed different people living in another age. To understand the Bible in its own context is to allow the text the freedom to stand in its own right. People can then enter into what Karl Barth called "the strange new world of the Bible."[1] But we cannot enter into the world of the Bible without carrying with us many of the assumptions, concerns, and questions of our own world. In other words, the Bible must also be brought into the strange new world in which we live. Our situation has a word to speak as well. If the Bible is to be truly heard, we must be aware of those factors in our own situation that affect our hearing. What is needed is what some have called "ideological suspicion,"[2] to counteract the unconscious assumptions of our day. For example, in a rich male-dominated society we have often emphasized those sins of arrogance and assertiveness that relate to the abuse of human strength. These are not, however, the sins of the people, including women, who have lived in a subordinate position for a long time and are having to learn to be more assertive and to discover their own strength. Worship that regards these latter characteristics as sins debilitates those who need to affirm them in themselves. The consequence is that although the strong confess their arrogance, they continue to retain their position of dominance.

Our own situation, however, can affect our hearing positively as well as negatively. The question has been raised in our time: "What does the gospel sound like from the side of the poor?" This acknowledges that the dominant interpretation has primarily arisen in the affluent West and in a segment of that society which is not poor. This question of interpretation becomes a question put to the churches as to whether they are in the right place and include the right people for hearing an authentic word. The well established and complacent are not well placed for hearing the word of the cross that calls for openness and vulnerability. The poor have more kinship with that word. One of the marks of authentic Christian community, referred to earlier, now comes into play. The inclusivity of the community determines the authenticity of its interpretation of the scriptures. Many sorts and conditions of people can ensure a breadth of awareness that enriches the church's hearing of the Word.

Who the congregation is and what it brings to its meeting under the Word are therefore decisive. The commitments and concerns of the congregation in its outreach ministry are not only subsequent to hearing the Word, but also prerequisites for hearing it anew. Bible study groups in congregations should be closely associated with or include those groups or individuals who are most committed to outreach. If prayer is an expression for the openness and vulnerability toward the world that characterizes Christian outreach, I can here affirm a necessary link between Bible study and prayer. In the liturgy, proclamation of the Word is both preceded and followed by prayer. This reflects the need for preparation for the reading and preaching in prayer and outreach and points to what necessarily follows them in the praise and outreach ministry of the congregation.

Prayer and proclamation belong together. The hearing of the Word, which takes place in prayer as a waiting upon God, is a congregational activity and also a vocation of the presider and preacher. The preacher is charged by the people to be a servant of the Word and, therefore, a spokesperson for God in addressing the people in the worship assembly. The preacher is also a spokesperson for the people, having been placed in the position as pastor not only to speak an individual word, but also to represent the people out of a knowledge of their experience gained in the exercise of pastoral responsibilities. A larger experience than that of one individual is brought to bear on the text. This is what makes preaching different from personal witness. Authentic preaching depends on the vital link between the text and the situation of the people discerned in pastoral care and involvement in the ordinary life of the world. The weekly cycle of listening to the text and listening to the people in pastoral care enters into the preacher's prayer and meditation before preaching. This is the spiritual discipline of the preacher as the crucible for the Word and for the experiences of the people. The preacher cannot live a cloistered existence with the spiritual discipline of a monk or a nun. That is an entirely different calling. Nor can the preacher spend a large part of the week holed up in a study and cut off from all human contact while producing a weekly masterpiece, as many of the "great" preachers have done. Such a preacher is bound to become hard of hearing with regard both to the word of scripture and to the voice of the people.

I have been speaking of the hearing of scripture as interpretation. Interpretation takes place within a movement from the text to our situation and back to the text. This movement is called a hermeneutical circle. The circle comprises both a hermeneutical function of the situation, in affecting how the text will be understood, and a hermeneutical function of the text, in opening up a new understanding of our situation. It is not enough, therefore, to speak only of interpreting the text. The goal of the text is not to be interpreted, but to interpret us.[3] This is the active, transforming role of the text at the root of dynamic preaching. Preaching, according to the hermeneutical scholar Gerhard Ebeling, is not only an exposition of the text; it is also its execution.[4]

It was Karl Barth who said that the preacher should prepare the sermon with the Bible in one hand and a newspaper in the other. This acknowledges the importance for preaching of knowing our situation. And yet Barth did not see the movement of the sermon as between the text and our situation, but rather from the beginning of the text to its end, with little asides addressing our situation.[5] For Barth, the hermeneutical circle existed apart from the situation of the hearer. In order to hear one has to take the leap of faith into the circle.[6] The circle, however, includes the situation of the hearer, which is not different from the situation of the unbeliever. Whereas Barth characterized preaching as proclamation of the Word, I consider it as both proclamation and response. Within the meeting under the Word it is the focal point or place where proclamation and response come together. This dynamic needs to be taken into account within the sermon.

Recognizing the involvement of the people in the preaching of the Word, Fred Craddock has proposed an inductive rather than deductive method in preaching. The inductive approach involves a process of mutual discovery between the preacher and the people rather than positing an authoritative proposition at the outset, from which certain inevitable conclusions can be drawn. This inductive approach accounts for the suggestive title of Craddock's book: *As One Without Authority*.[7] The book challenges the authoritative stance of preaching that has had the effect of making people passive. It elevates the people to a position of participants rather than consigning them to the role of passive listeners only.

This is a valuable concern. But using an analogy from scientific method does not quite fit what happens in preaching. It fails to take adequate account of the givenness of the text whose authority is acknowledged by both the preacher and the people. The preacher does have the authority of the text behind what he or she says as long as he or she remains under the Word and neither claims prerogatives over it nor provides a substitute for it in some article of personal or conventional wisdom.

What the preacher has to do is to bring the text into the sermon so that it can be heard, albeit at first in only a preliminary way. The preacher has to tell the story according to the text. This is often best done by capturing a dominant metaphor or motif from the text rather than repeating and embellishing it unduly as if it has not already been read. Different motifs, of course, can emerge on different occasions. This is why the text has proved to be inexhaustible for preaching. Other riches of the text can be brought in later in the sermon in support of the chosen motif. The preacher, for example, preaching on the parable of the prodigal son, might fruitfully focus on the dynamic interchange between the father and the elder brother—"This your son . . ." "This your brother . . ."—in order to capture what is at stake in the loving relationship between father and prodigal and elder son depicted in the parable. The rest of the parable and indeed the other lectionary readings can cast additional light on the chosen motif. It is certainly not advisable to preach equally on all three lectionary readings!

The preacher next has the task of bringing about an intersection between the text and the situation of the people. Here again metaphors and stories can evoke in lively fashion the lives of the people so that they can recognize themselves and, as it were, say "That's it exactly!" or "Amen." Metaphors, as John D. Crossan has pointed out, do not only inform; they enable participation.[8] It is the intention of this part of the sermon to capture the lives of the people that they may be drawn into the sermon as active participants. Metaphors enable this participation of the people better than merely alluding to their situation or trying to deal with it exhaustively or analytically. Nor does the sermon mainly deal with problems, as Harry Emerson Fosdick maintained. Its task is rather to illuminate and transform life.

If, for example, the preacher wants to take account of the unemployment many people are suffering, she or he can do so, not merely by alluding to the problems of the unemployed or seeking to analyze the economic situation with a view to uncovering the causes of unemployment. Rather, the preacher will draw on her or his knowledge of the actual lives of unemployed people—gathered in the exercise of pastoral responsibilities—to depict in metaphor and story the anxieties, hopes, and feelings of worthlessness and futility of the unemployed. The aim of the story is that the unemployed themselves will feel that they are truly represented and that the employed will have their sensitivities awakened to people in more trying circumstances than their own.

Such stories will always be descriptive in tone, never judgmental. It is often difficult in telling stories to avoid pejorative over-tones. This must be avoided. Unfortunately perhaps because of the usual absence of children during the sermon time, preachers commonly make jokes at their expense in a sermon or describe adult weaknesses with pejorative references to childhood, such as "being childish" or being selfish like a spoiled child. The in-creasingly vocal women's movement has begun to make it unac-ceptable to make sexist jokes or similar stereotyped remarks about women's experience. It helps to believe that you are actually talking to the people whose lives are under consideration. So much the better, therefore, if the congregation is inclusive enough or has a wide enough outreach to include a great breadth of human experiences.

Furthermore, the preacher must seek to be comprehensive in bringing the people's situation to expression. If children's experi-ences, for example, were adequately evoked in the sermon by story and metaphor, would there be any need to send them away after a brief children's time, as is the usual practice in many churches? This ritual of "sending them away," it may be said in passing, looks suspiciously like what the disciples were advocating to Jesus, who responded in opposite fashion: "Let the children come to me." Women's experience, too, has been notoriously absent from male-dominated preaching. In my own experience of preaching classes that included significant numbers of female preachers, it has been startling to hear a whole range of human experience addressed that I was unaccustomed to hearing about in worship.

Dwelling on certain issues and situations to the exclusion of others can also distort the liturgy and antagonize the people. Some preachers, for instance, think almost exclusively in terms of per-sonal needs, leaving out of account the larger social implications of the faith. Others are so social-action-oriented that they forget that people can be suffering agonizing pain and that that, too, needs to be addressed by the healing Word of the gospel. A helpful guide for preachers can be found in the four categories of the Prayers of the People that most service books recommend. The categories, which are meant to cover the whole range of life, include world, church, local community, and personal needs. Given the close connection between the sermon and the Prayers of the People, it is natural that the concerns that they address will coincide to a considerable degree.

The theological category for our human situation as it enters into the sermon is law. Tillich referred to law as "mirror of existence."[9] Ebeling has characterized it as "man's being as it in fact is."[10] Ebeling can also, with reference to God, speak of law as God's question put to human existence or simply as the "questionableness of existence."[11] This was encountered earlier in the Genesis account of Adam and Eve's flight from God and God's question to them, "Where are you?" This searching question is the cutting edge of the reality of our situation that preaching exposes. As Herman G. Stuempfle Jr. has written in *Preaching Law and Gospel*, "It is part of the function of preaching to lay bare this situation with such clarity that it will be impossible for us to escape into any of the false secular or religious securities which beckon us."[12]

Beside this preaching of the law as "mirror of existence" Stuempfle sets Luther's understanding of the law as a "hammer of judgment"[13] that drives the sinner to repentance. Rather than separating these two functions in preaching, I would maintain that no bigger hammer is needed to convince people of the extremity of their situation than simply to confront people with its reality. Where words of judgment are called for, the preacher must always speak them as one who is under the same condemnation or necessity as the rest of the people.

Whereas the law prescribes the limits of our situation, the gospel presents its possibilities. These possibilities can be opened in preaching, with reference to our past as forgiveness and to our future as a new vision of what God has in store for us. If the question of the law is "Where are you?" the question of the gospel is "Where is Jesus?" for Jesus is the One in whom, as the Christ, new life is to be found. This is the Christ of faith who is sought, not the Jesus of two thousand years ago. Both questions, therefore, require a diligent search of ourselves and of the world we live in. At first there can be quite a discrepancy between the answers to the two questions, but ultimately the answer to the second becomes the answer to the first when the sinner who is hiding from God can come out of hiding and confidently say, "I am in Christ."

It must be remembered, however, in order that this language not be a cloak for self-serving piety, that the Risen One who is with us to be heard and seen is always the Crucified One.[14] Only the person who suffers with Christ in response to the command "Follow me" can say, "I am in Christ." It is to be expected that being in and with Christ will require a considerable dislocation in a person's life, contrary to the easy assurance of some Christians who are all too quick to witness to the presence of Jesus in their lives, as if Jesus were always at their beck and call. To be with Jesus means going out to those who are weak and oppressed as the ones with whom he identified himself through his suffering on the cross. It is fully in keeping, therefore, with the gospel to see the Christ in our midst in the face of a child, or a woman, or in the faces of any of the rejected ones in our society.

I will show how law and gospel function in relation to each other in preaching as I turn now to consider what happens when text and situation meet in the sermon. When text and situation intersect in the sermon, the word of the text will appear at first as a weak word beside the word from our situation that is reinforced by the conventional wisdom about our experience and by the power of all the media of communication. This word from our situation is not yet the mirror of existence that reveals its full reality; that is, it is not yet perceived as law. The juxtaposition of weak word and situation enforced by conventional wisdom may prompt the people to question the text: "How can that be?" This question, too, should enter into the sermon. The preacher should not seek to make the text easy to believe by minimizing the discrepancy between the text's word and the word of our situation. This discrepancy builds the tension that can bring about a transformation to seeing the situation in a new light. Only with the help of the text is the situation finally revealed in its true light and the law is heard. At this point the listener becomes more amenable to hearing the gospel. The movement of hearing the gospel comes in the form of a "twist" or "reversal."

Crossan has spoken of this power of reversal in Jesus' parables.

His parables are metaphors of the reign of God that not only point to its coming, but are also part of its advent. In the parables God's reign comes with all its power to transform and make new. This is not the power of sheer force. It is the power that is realized in weakness after the manner of the cross of Christ.

So the preacher may stack up against the weak word of the text, or what Luther in his hymn "A Mighty Fortress Is Our God" called "one little word," all the power and authority of the wisdom of the world. The promise of the text is that God's Word, which is no more than the weakness and foolishness of the cross, will prevail. In the intersection between text and situation, therefore, the preacher needs only to make room for a full and genuine response of the people to take place. Let their hopes be expressed, their fears, their joys, their disappointments and despair, their illusions and their unbelief. Preaching is not a pious act. Let the law that is the mirror of their existence and may become the hammer of judgment be seen and felt. Only in the face of this seemingly inescapable law can the gospel be heard as a word of grace that opens up a new future and a hope. The inescapability of the law is shown with absolute clarity in Jesus' teaching. In the Sermon on the Mount Jesus sharpened the commandment against killing to include "every one who is angry with his brother [Matt. 5:22]." When he said, "It is easier for a camel to go through the eye of a needle than for a rich man to enter the kingdom of God," the disciples "were greatly astonished, saying, 'Who then can be saved?' [Matt. 19:24–25]." It is this question, with its utter letting go of any presumption to righteousness, that opens the way for Jesus' grace-filled answer: "With people this is impossible, but with God all things are possible [v. 26]." It is on this promise, after all other options have been closed, that preaching depends.

Luther believed that law and gospel fight it out every week in the sermon.[15] If the proper tension has developed in the sermon, when the gospel triumphs it is going to be a surprise rather than a foregone conclusion. And when the gospel word is proclaimed it is more likely to come first as a tentative proposal, a mere question, "Could it be that . . . ?" or an exclamation, "The amazing thing is that . . . ," rather than as a conclusive argument.

What follows is not further confirmation by means of argument of the truth of the gospel, but rather a simple invitation. The goal of the sermon is to open new doors and invite people to enter. The people are empowered to enter by the gospel that has emerged out of the conflict with the law. Here, after the gospel has been preached, comes another use of the law—what Calvin called its third use.[16] The law now becomes the guide to the way people have to go. Of this transformed law that follows the gospel Barth has said: "God's commandment is permission."[17] As such it is not contrary to freedom, but what makes freedom possible, because the people need help in living the new life of faith. The freedom of the gospel in a sermon may often be expressed as a joyful "Now you can" or "Yes you may" rather than as the grim "You must" of the law that existed before the gospel. The latter is law because it calls for an action on the part of the hearer that it does not enable. It is a word that leads to despair rather than offers hope because it does not offer what it demands. The gospel, or the word of the transformed law after the gospel, on the contrary, is one of empowerment for action that goes beyond the circumscribed limits of what was possible before. The promise of the resurrection, which accompanies the word of the cross, opens the way to an entirely new future. The sermon invites the hearer into that future as a call to the new life of faith.

But what is this new life of faith like? Where does it lead? The preacher can offer help here again with the use of story and metaphor. This time the preacher draws on the experience of faith of all ages. The people are part of a communion of saints that extends into all ages—figures both great and small. The Jesus of history, as the pioneer of faith, becomes a model that reveals how the freedom of faith can be lived.[18] But so does the neighbor woman who is struggling with her children to make ends meet but has room in her heart for caring for other children besides her own, or the businessperson who is concerned about where her or his company is investing its money that it not contribute to a repressive situation. These examples of faith both inspire and offer direction for people who accept the invitation of the gospel.

But the sermon does not complete the invitation or fully work out its implications. The movement of the liturgy allows for further working out of its implication in the Responses to the Word and in the Prayers of the People, in which the people themselves can voice what they see the implications of the gospel to be for the outreach of the church. It is of great importance for the movement of the liturgy that the Prayers of the People be restored to their place after the sermon where they can form a dialogue with the sermon. This dialogue is greatly enhanced when a different voice than the preacher's leads the prayers. Then the Service of the Table offers the opportunity to confirm one's faith by accepting the invitation to the Table. Sermons that allow for this movement of the liturgy could be considerably briefer than the twenty-five or thirty minutes that are thought necessary in many preaching-oriented churches. Preaching does not need to be the full *son et lumière* performance that it often seeks to be if there are other vivid and involving portions of the service.

The value of the full eucharistic act of worship as a context for preaching cannot be overestimated. Nothing could be more appropriate after the proclamation of the Word than a procession of thankful people going forward to the Table in response to the invitation. This is the goal of the sermon that points beyond the sermon itself to the communion at the Lord's Table as a sign of the reign of God into which Christians are called to enter. I wonder if the absence of such a culmination of the Service of the Word in an invitation to the Table and the actual response of going forward was sensed by revivalist religion with its altar call and sawdust trail. Does truly evangelical faith require the opportunity on the part of individuals to assent to the gospel preached by some appropriate liturgical response? The problem with revivalism was its individualistic and pietistic conception of that response. A person goes forward for the salvation of his or her own soul. But the invitation to the Table is one that calls the person to be remade in the image of God as part of Christ's Body, the church.

Have the sermons in many Protestant churches, where the Eucharist is not celebrated weekly, had a tendency to be inconclusive, without the evangelical urgency in calling for a change of life as intrinsic to what it means to be a Christian? Here I am not speaking of the need only for once-and-for-all conversions, but of the need to be tugged back week by week to our Christian calling. Every sermon should call for a change of life and issue in an invitation to accept that new option for oneself. There is an intimate link between the proclamation of the Word and the invitation to the Table that is disrupted when the latter does not occur.

Does not the prophetic character of preaching also suffer in the absence of the Eucharist? I have already alluded to the social implications of the meal as a sign-act that challenges the status quo and calls us into the future God has in store for the world. Without this impetus, does preaching tend to become complacent—a mere reflection of current values? Historically this appears to be a common failing of Protestant preaching. Or, as a corollary, it becomes moralistic, urging people to be better than they are without empowering them to be so. Neither the offering of false comfort nor moralistic exhortation approach the prophetic preaching of Jesus that overturns the world as it is and creates a new world. Preachers who seek to be prophetic in radical ways all too often suffer the pain of seeing their congregations fragmented by their efforts. The option they are left with is to either tone down their prophetic concern or move to another congregation. Could this lamentable state of affairs, in which the cutting edge of the gospel is blunted, be overcome by a regular celebration of the sacrament of unity? This unity at the Table does not paper over our differences. It helps us to love one another in our differences as we experience our oneness in the Body of Christ. Such a unifying event as the regular culmination of our services of worship would surely go far toward creating the loving community we are called to be.

Without the regular sacrament of communion have the Protestant churches called on the sermon to do too much in their worship services? Preachers strive through their spoken word to awaken people to a keen sense of the presence of God in their lives and of their own place in God's purposes for the world. But the result often is a sermon that attempts too much and achieves too little. The preacher is disappointed because the people don't seem to respond well to what he or she is saying. And the people are disappointed because they have been unmoved by what they have heard. And the lament goes up to heaven once again that preaching is losing its power!

What do we do? Do we hone our preaching skills and double

our effort? This might be highly desirable in some cases! But might it not be worth considering whether the context in which preaching takes place has a bearing on the effectiveness of the act? I have already spoken of the importance of the congregation's makeup and concerns as a context for hearing and preaching the Word. Worship, too, is a context that is often overlooked by preachers who are preoccupied with their own part in the service. Worship, as Leander Keck has said, provides an "interpretive matrix" for preaching.[19] Preaching, in other words, is a liturgical act, and has its proper place within the movement of a service that includes both spoken word and word enacted.

God's Word comes to us in the spoken word, which Luther called the *viva vox Dei* (the living Word of God), as personal address, as one human being speaking to another. With all the doubts in recent years about the sermon as an effective means of communication, we have often forgotten its liturgical significance as personal address in a context in which it is followed by an *act* of communion or communication. No technician could devise a more effective multimedia event than that which may occur between pulpit and Table. And in an age when our ears are bombarded by a cacophony of sound might it not be that a simple word, truly spoken, addressing us personally, is what we all most need and long to hear? We want to be named, to have our name called out in the crowd—as frightening and full of promise as that can be.

In the liturgy such a word may be spoken, not in exalted tones, nor even with the high art of the orator or actor speaking her or his lines, but in an ordinary voice that points to the reality of our situation before God as seen in the light of scripture. P. T. Forsyth wrote: "The cure for pulpit dullness is not brilliancy, as in literature. It is reality."[20] The sermon, surrounded by the full splendor of the liturgy, including the Lord's Supper, can be about the true business of pointing us to that reality.

10

The Service of the Table: Honoring Gifts

In the Service of the Word, as we have seen, the movement is first from God to us, followed by our response. The Service of the Table begins with us and culminates in an act of communion wherein we are united with God and with one another in preparation for living out the freedom of our faith in the world as members of Christ's Body. The movement of gathering and sending forth comes to a conclusion when the meal is eaten and the table is cleared. The priest's words at the conclusion of the Latin mass were all that were necessary: *"Ita missa est"* (sometimes translated as "Go; the church is sent"). Our worship continues in our daily life. The Service of the Table is done in obedience to Jesus' command "Do this in remembrance of me." Its words and actions follow those of Jesus' last meal with his disciples in the Upper Room, expressed in the four verbs "take," "bless," "break," and "give." (1 Corinthians 11:23-26; Mark 14:22-25; Matthew 26:26-29) Hence we *present* our gifts, join the great Prayer of *Thanksgiving*, *break* the bread and pour the wine, and *share* the bread and the cup with one another.

In some traditions, before gifts are brought forward, the people make their *peace* with one another in accord with the scriptural injunction in Matthew 5:23-24 that calls for being reconciled. This action, which was reduced to a word formula, is being recovered, either in this place, before the presenting of the gifts, or later, before communion, as a genuine opportunity within the service for loving and reconciling actions to take place. Such action is facilitated if the people are standing and able to move around freely rather than being confined to greeting only those in a neighboring pew. Furthermore, the meaning of the exchange of peace should always be kept clear. It is not a time for casual conversation.

The *Presenting of the Gifts* has been called "the liturgy of the people" because it constitutes an offering of the people's lives, the very stuff of their worldly existence, at the Table, there to be transformed for the salvation of the world. The action should, therefore, be highlighted in the service with a procession of gifts from among the people, including both the money offering and the bread and wine for communion. It is not appropriate, however, to elevate the gifts in procession as if they are already Christ's body and blood.

The *Great Thanksgiving* or *Eucharistic Prayer* is the moment in the liturgy when the Christian community affirms its identity by rehearsing the story of faith in an act of praise. God is blessed, after the manner of Jewish blessings (the *Berakoth*), by remembering God's saving acts. The prayer moves in the sequence of the story of salvation from creation to redemption to anticipation of the fulfillment of God's will and purpose for the world. As such it reveals the close link between proclamation and praise. As with the historic credal statements, the prayer is trinitarian in shape, although it is addressed to the first person of the Trinity throughout. This prayer is said by the presider, as the one who has been authorized to speak for both God and people, and is joined by the people in their acclamations. Presider and people continue in prayer together after the Great Thanksgiving with the Lord's Prayer.

After the Eucharistic Prayer the bread is broken (the *Fraction*) and the wine poured. When the table is ready and the servers are prepared to serve, the people are invited to come forward to share in the meal fellowship. In this action of *koinonia* (communion) the people are united with one another and with God as the community of the New Age, the church, by which God's saving action will be witnessed to and furthered in the world. The *Sending Forth* concludes the service as the people turn outward to their lives in the world.

The sketch of the movement of the Service of the Table needs the kind of elaboration that many handbooks on worship provide. On paper it looks rather inconsequential. But that is because there can be no substitute for the sign-acts themselves. These sign-acts have the quality of metaphors that speak for themselves. A book on liturgical theology cannot re-create the experience of the metaphors; it can only, like a work of literary criticism, seek to explain how the metaphors function.

The sacraments are, for Christians, metaphors of God's presence. James White, in his book on sacraments, has designated them as God's self-giving.[1] The Lord's Supper is a metaphor of the community realized through the action of Jesus Christ reconciling us to one another and to God. As such, it is a sign of perfect community—a community that far outreaches the community we experience with one another. When we gather at the Lord's Table we are united with Christians of all ages—past, present, and future—the communion of saints. It is a table, we believe, from which, ultimately, no one will be excluded. It is the heavenly feast that God has in store for the whole world. We need signs and metaphors in worship that unite us with one another. But more important, these metaphors point beyond our world to God. They enable us to express what our hope is and to experience a foretaste of the future we anticipate in hope. And this future is assured in the promise we receive through our memory of Jesus' life, death, and rising again. Our sacrament, therefore, is a sign of both memory and hope.

And so, at the Table, we learn what real community is. We learn by experiencing a foretaste of it. This is true for children and adults alike. Both are capable of wonder, love, and praise. But this foretaste whets our appetite. It raises our consciousness; it offers us a new vision of the world. Caught by this vision we can no longer acquiesce in the way things are—in the world's lack of community, in the injustices whereby some benefit at the expense of others, in the enmity, prejudice, and fear that lie at the root of our alienation from one another. In the sacraments we are commissioned to, and empowered for, a new engagement with the world that is characterized by faith, love, and joy, rather than by self-serving and despair.

I have earlier examined the power of metaphors to evoke another world. But how does this actually happen in the meal fellowship of Christians? I know of no clearer portrayal of the power of the meal metaphor than the remarkable film entitled *The Last Supper*,[2] by the Cuban, Marxist film director Tomas Gutierrez Alea. The film is both a sharp indictment of the hypocrisy of the piety that often prevails in Christian worship, and a witness to the power of that worship to do the unexpected and the transforming, despite the intention of the participants.

The setting of the story is a Cuban slave plantation in the nineteenth century. The absentee landowner returns to the plantation during Holy Week, resolved, because of remorse for some personal failings, to reenact, as an act of penance, the events of the original Holy Week with his slaves. With the compliance of the local priest, a well-intentioned but ineffectual man, he selects twelve slaves and proceeds with the action of washing their feet and sharing with them the meal in the Upper Room. As the master, he sees himself in the role of Christ. The slaves, cast as the disciples, react with amused bewilderment and desire no more than to make the most of a good time.

During the meal the master seeks to edify his slaves with a homily on the Christian virtues and rewards of being a good slave and suffering one's lot with patience and humility. As the meal progresses the good food and wine produce a sufficient bond among the participants that the slaves confide in their owner about the hardship they suffer at the hands of their brutal overseer. The master commiserates with them to the extent of promising them the next day, Good Friday, as a holiday.

But the next day, in the slaveowner's absence, the overseer demands that the slaves work as usual, contrary to the master's promise. The disillusioned slaves rebel. When the owner hears what has happened he reacts with outrage and immediately sets out to quell the insurrection with all the vicious force he can muster. But before he does so there is a significant little interchange between himself and the priest. "How, after all the kindness I have shown these slaves and what I have taught them," the owner asks, "can they show such ingratitude?" To this the priest responds: "You may have thought last night that you were winning them over by talking to them about the Christian virtues of a good slave. But what they were really learning was what it is like to eat at the master's table." Here, remarkably, a non-Christian Marxist film director witnesses to the power of the metaphor of the Eucharist to make people free.

If, indeed, metaphors speak for themselves, as this film indicates, we have to look into the adequacy of the sign-acts of the Eucharist, as they occur in the churches, to see if they say what is intended. The question of format (or what James White calls "the quality of the celebration"[3]), therefore, cannot be avoided in considering what happens in the Service of the Table. We have already observed a significant convergence occurring among the churches that is especially marked by the recovery of the sacraments as metaphors or sign-acts. This recovery entails different things in different churches. It is occurring in most Protestant churches within a heritage of a loss of symbol and metaphor occasioned by the Reformers' attempts to cleanse the church from abuses of the sacramental system in the Middle Ages. In the Roman Catholic Church and in others that have retained a high liturgical tradition the recovery involves a simplification, as Vatican II put it, of an overly elaborate liturgy. This simplification is necessary in order to let the symbols speak for themselves, instead of being treated allegorically or having magical properties ascribed to them.

Allegory differs from symbol in the way its meaning is conceived. Paul Ricoeur has said about myth: "It means what it says." A symbol or myth discloses its meaning, whereas allegory has its meaning assigned to it. In allegory the meaning is hidden unless it is translated. And then the allegory, as Ricoeur says, "falls away like a useless garment."[4] Worship becomes allegorical when it accumulates a plethora of hidden meanings beyond what the symbols themselves signify. Worship as allegory can be a means of retaining power among an elite, in this case the clergy, who alone have knowledge of the secret meanings. The restoration of the symbols, by letting them speak for themselves, therefore, becomes a means of empowering the whole group.

Magic also takes power away from the participant, by ascribing to the symbols a mysterious property *in themselves* to effect changes. Magic differs from the dynamic quality of symbols being considered here in locating the power of the symbol *in itself*, rather than in

141

the interaction *between* those whom the symbol joins. Bread that is too holy to be touched by nonpriestly hands is magical. Bread that can be shared is a symbol of love.

If the so-called liturgical churches need to simplify their liturgy in order to recover its symbolic nature, the "nonliturgical" churches need to recover a conscious use of symbols in worship. I say "conscious use" because worship is always symbolic whether we intend it or not. If we are not conscious of symbols that are there, our worship often conveys conflicting messages. This happens, for instance, when the preacher speaks of the nearness of God from a high platform, or when the importance of Holy Communion is spoken of in a church in which the altar-table is dwarfed by other furnishings. What is at stake in the ecumenical convergence among the churches toward a recovery of symbol or metaphor in worship is the full participation of the whole people of God in worship and their empowerment for Christian living in the world.

The recovery of the full symbolic impact of the liturgy cannot occur, however, without a renewal in how the word enters the service in reading, preaching, and prayer. We noted a corresponding need, when examining the Service of the Word, for a recovery of the full action of the Eucharist as a context for effective preaching. Word and Table exist in mutual interdependence.

The importance of the Word for the sacrament can be seen in Augustine's dictum that the word comes to the element and then there is a sacrament.[5] This dependence on accompanying word would appear to conflict with the claim that symbols speak for themselves. Words, indeed, cannot make symbols speak anything other than what they, in their intrinsic nature, can speak. The symbols of worship have been chosen for their appropriateness to the gospel. Like gestures, their intention is evident in themselves and does not differ inside or outside the context of worship. Nevertheless, symbols share with all human experience the quality of ambiguity that arises out of the possibility of deception inherent in a fallen creation. As Ricoeur has noted: "All phenomenology develops in this enchanted precinct of vanity, under the category of the *Pseudo.* That is why no phenomenology, no science of appearances, can take the place of a critique of the illusion of appearance."[6] The deceptive quality of evil is a familiar notion in the history of religion. In the book of Revelation the fallen Babylon resembles the New Jerusalem, and in Edmund Spenser's *Faerie Queene*, evil, although no match for the good, always masquerades as the good and attempts to win through deception. An embrace, then, is a sign of love, unless it is done to deceive. A shared cup is a sign of community, unless it is a cup of poison. Within the liturgy, however, the accompanying word furthers the true intention of the symbol or sign-act that it can be known not simply as a present happening among human beings, fraught with ambiguity, but also as a communion with God and with people in all ages. Attached to the symbol is the Word of promise that, with the enlivening Spirit, calls forth belief.

The readings, the sermon, and the Great Prayer of Thanksgiving show that the sign-acts of the Eucharist are occurring within the context of the history of salvation and are indeed an event in that history. The word makes explicit the beyond of the symbol in terms of the Christian story of faith. A theology of the sacraments and symbols, therefore, must go beyond a mere anthropology of the origin of symbols in natural gestures and sign-acts. It is only with word and sign-act together that we have a sacrament.

The accompanying word also guards against a danger in the power of symbols—that their power can mistakenly be ascribed to the symbols themselves, making them idolatrous. I have noted this tendency in the discussion of magic in worship. If symbols are not to become idols they must be broken by the word. The symbols in Christian worship, as Paul Tillich noted, must always be broken symbols. They must be cracked open in order to reveal their personal, social, and political meaning. The words and symbols have their meaning only in relation to how the church lives its life in the world where God is at work. Preaching can be said, therefore, to demythologize the sacraments by preventing them from becoming a timeless sacred ceremony apart from daily life.

Indeed the ritual of the Eucharist enacts this breaking of the symbols in the breaking of bread and pouring out of wine. They are there not to be adored, but to be consumed. Like the manna in the wilderness, they cannot be preserved. It is this brokenness of the symbols that not only enables them to be shared, but also connects them with God's saving action on the cross. The preaching of Christ crucified makes explicit for our understanding this connection between the sign-acts of worship and God's saving action in history. At the same time it calls for our participation in this saving action of God by giving ourselves in acts of loving service. The church itself, then, becomes a sacrament to the world[7] in acting out God's self-giving love for the world.

All that has been said about the word that accompanies the symbol does not detract from the power of symbols to speak for themselves. Looking more closely at actual liturgies in the churches, we have to raise questions, then, about matters of format and procedure. We have to examine the symbols for their theological impact. The practice of preparing the altar-table for the eucharistic meal without any participation of the people in a presentation of their gifts, for example, indicates, not that it is the substance of their lives that is being transformed in the communion, but that they are merely recipients of a grace being bestowed from above. The kind of bread and wine also has to be considered. Could the people's contribution be more genuinely expressed by the bread and wine they make than by the more refined commercial products, be they little cubes of white bread or communion wafers, that appear not to have been ever touched by human hands? The practice of substituting grape juice for wine, in my opinion, is also a doubtful one. In choosing the elements of bread and wine Jesus did not seek to purify them before blessing them, as we tend to do, when we opt for vitamin-enriched white bread, or for grape juice instead of wine. The bread and wine are signs of our ordinary life in all its ambiguity. That common life is hallowed when the bread and wine are brought forward to the Table to be consecrated as signs of Jesus' body and blood.

The manner of distributing the elements also must come under scrutiny. The utter passivity of receiving the bread directly into the mouth from the hand of the priest instead of hand to hand in an act of sharing has already been alluded to. Nor does the practice of the people receiving the elements, including separate little glasses of grape juice, while sitting in their pews, adequately signify a community gathered in praise and thanksgiving at the Table. It is still more a matter of reception by, rather than an action of, the people. People customarily stand to praise God. Is it not, therefore, also appropriate to stand for the central action of the service of thanksgiving? So when we are invited to come to the Table, ought we not to leave our seats and actually go, forming a procession of thankful people? This action may occur in good time and with as little regimentation as possible when more than one station is provided to which the people may go. The servers may include the presiding minister, assistants, and other members of the baptized, with care being taken to include various kinds of people representing the whole community, young and old, female and male, and so on.

Resistance to this kind of participation often emerges in no small measure because it evokes a spirituality of communion contrary to the one that people have been accustomed to. Standing instead of sitting or kneeling does denote a different attitude. Joining a procession that leads to a gathering at the altar-table does interfere with private meditation. Being called on to take part instead of simply receiving or even adoring at a distance does constitute a different understanding of holiness and grace. With the change of format and use of symbols and metaphors a new spirituality of communion is emerging. The sacred is now being experienced in the hospitality of the Table and the familiar act of sharing instead of in holy distance with objects too sacred to be touched. The Service of the Table is becoming a communion time instead of an occasion for private prayer, a time of rejoicing as well as of penitence, a time for empowerment for living in the world, rather than a quiet refuge from the world.

There are indeed many obstacles in the way of this kind of communion at the Table. We have considered such factors as clericalism and an entrenched passivity among the people. We have observed the loss of symbolism in the churches either through overly elaborate liturgies or through an excess of puritan reaction against the use of visual signs and images. Two practical matters loom very large in the question of whether the churches can recover a liturgy that enables the full participation of the people in a service of both word and sacrament. One has to do with the buildings we worship in, and the other with the size of many worship assemblies.

Many church buildings are ill-suited for the kinds of actions of the people we have been describing. There is simply not enough room at the front of the church for people to gather. Or there are too many obstacles placed in their way, such as large, overbearing pulpits and forbidding railings separating the chancel and the nave; narrow aisles between rows of pews that restrict movement; an altar-table at a great distance from the people and joined to the nave only by a narrow passageway between rows of choir stalls. What these churches express in their architecture—yes, buildings are symbols that speak to us too—is a worship that separates the sacred from the secular, the clergy from the rest of the baptized, and reinforces the notion that the congregation is there only to receive and not also to participate. Most congregations are not in a position to go out and build a new church according to order. Nor do they need to! Effective revisions are often being made to existing spaces without exorbitant cost, because most changes involve, not the addition of costly furnishings, but the removal of them. What is being sought is space at the front that includes table and lectern and plenty of room for the people to gather. This space should be in proximity to where the people are seated.

Perhaps the most difficult space to work with liturgically, therefore, is the long narrow rectangle. This shape is often justified by appeal to the importance of a directional sense in worship. Worship calls us to look beyond ourselves. As true as this is, the direction for worship is easily established by the people facing one way toward the table, pulpit, or font. This direction could change according to the kind of service, or even during a service, such as when Baptism is celebrated within the Eucharist, if the seating arrangements were flexible enough to permit such changes. Distance does not need to be a factor in establishing direction. Indeed, as a general rule, the closer people are to the object of their attention, the greater will be the impact of that object on them.

But even long rectangles are being made suitable for worship. Many of the best spatial renovations have been accomplished by dividing a long nave into two portions with a movable partition. One portion is where the people assemble for worship, and the other is a meeting room or concourse where the people can gather before or after worship, or assemble for meetings. This forecourt, which is not unlike an atrium in an early Roman church, provides a transitional space between the worship and the congregation's life in the world. When larger-than-normal assemblies occur the whole space can be opened up.

One of the most attractive settings for worship I have experienced is an old Gothic-style church that had been renovated with little cost to the congregation. They had simply changed the direction of worship by placing table and lectern along a side wall on which a large wooden cross was hung. The pews were rearranged in a U-shape to create an open space around the altar-table in which people could gather at communion time. If this congregation had had the money, they would probably have replaced the pews with more flexible seating arrangements. But lacking it they nonetheless were able to create, with existing furnishings, an entirely new sense of space. Most striking for me in the services I have attended there is the strong impact of both the words and the signs, enabled by the proximity of all the people to the worship center and to one another. Also our nearness to one another and the ease with which we could move toward one another gave me the sense, as a stranger, of being accepted into the community as a friend.

This was a congregation of some one hundred to one hundred fifty persons. Whether such a community experience or effect of word and symbol can occur in a large, more impersonal gathering is the second question we have to consider. Greater numbers and greater distance usually go hand in hand. Too often the person who enters as a stranger also leaves as a stranger. Is such a distance from one another and from the sacramental signs fatal to eucharistic celebration?

Large, impersonal assemblies may, indeed, be one of the major obstacles to the recovery of a fully participatory service of worship in word and sacrament. Not only is it a matter of the long time it takes for a large number to communicate. More important is the tendency of words and symbols to lose their impact, and thus their meaning, when heard or viewed from afar. It may be that there are times for large throngs of Christians, indeed numbers of congregations, to assemble in worship. The worship of multitudes, perhaps expressing the unity of congregations in a larger parish or pastoral zone, or the assembly of Christians with people of other faiths united in a common cause such as peace, can be an elevating sign of the extent and glory of God's reign in the world. But for the weekly Word and Table communion of Christians, worship might better take place in much smaller gatherings. Such an eventuality might be in store for Christians in the years ahead without any precipitous action on our part. We no longer live in an era when perhaps the best sign of the relationship between the church and a Christianized world was the open portal of a large hall of worship. If there is to be an effective interaction now between the churches and a largely indifferent society, it will be by invitation and out-reach. These are more likely to occur in an assembly in which each person's presence counts for something and in which to be absent is to be missed. Christian worship with full participation of the people calls for the sharing and honoring of people's gifts.

At the heart of our Christian community is the honoring of one another's gifts that receives its focus at the Table. It is what makes Christian faith and life distinctive. There is no grace or empower-ment in being merely recipients of special favors in a grand action of divine charity. We receive more honor than that in being called to offer ourselves as partners in God's plan and process of renewal in the world. The wonder and grace of it all is that God wishes to carry out God's creative and saving work, not without us, but with us! And therein is the meaning and purpose of our life as given by God.

But how can this be? The world's need is great and our offering is small. We can dare to claim such a meaning and purpose in our gifts only because of the measure that God uses in receiving them. This measure is not according to the world's scales that say this gift weighs more and this one less, but according to the measure of God, who looks into the heart of the giver to discern the value of rhe gift, even as Jesus did when he took special note of a poor widow's gift of two small coins to the temple treasury. "This poor widow," said Jesus, "put in more, more than those who had contributed out of their riches. For in her poverty she gave all she had!" All of us, according to this measure, have valuable gifts. And when we offer them to God and in God's service they go toward the upbuilding of the community and the well-being of the world. This is our Christian ministry—our liturgy.

In our Sunday liturgy we have the opportunity to put into

practice this distinctive way of acting. It is often noted that our word worship comes from the Anglo-Saxon *worthship*. In our worship we show forth God's worth in acts of praise and thanksgiving. But less often is recognized the surprising way in which this "worthship" extends also to ourselves. God honors us in accepting our gifts. This is the measure of God's grace to us, which we in turn may extend to one another as we honor one another's gifts. In such a way the church becomes a *community of shared gifts* because everyone's gift is honored.

And the wonderful thing is that in this community of shared gifts, we discover gifts that we didn't know we had before: gifts of loving that affect our relationships with others in the home and place of work; gifts of speaking that enable us to speak up in situations in which we would normally have maintained a timid silence; gifts of discernment that give us a different view of our world, opening our eyes to the inequities of our society and in our world; and gifts of courage to act in order to put things right. In honoring one another's gifts we become not only the community of shared gifts, but more, *the gifted community.* By some miracle we have more to give. Remember the story of the feeding of the five thousand. What the disciples have is a child's offering of five loaves and two fish. Not enough, if they simply passed them out to the crowd. But put in the hands of Jesus, a remarkable transformation takes place. The five loaves and two fish become enough and more. All are fed and some remains left over!

In the Eucharist we have the privilege of participating in this miracle. To the Table we bring our gifts of bread and wine—ordinary things. The bread is the staple of our lives, what we sweat to earn. But it is also the bread we deny to others, as many people in this world starve for want of it. With the wine we celebrate our joy in life and yet may drink it to our own destruction. These gifts of ours are ambivalent at best. But it is for this very reason that they express so well what is at the root of human existence.

God receives these gifts at the Table. And from that Table we receive them back again transformed! By some miracle they are transformed into a means of grace for us and for the whole world. They become to us Christ's very body, now the stuff of our own lives, our very selves renewed in the power of Christ's spirit within us. The bread and wine are signs to us, that we may become a sign to the world, of a love far greater than the world has ever known, a love that offers this world a future and a hope.

Our Christian story is one of God's redeeming love in the world. God overcomes the forces of evil and oppression by an act of suffering love in solidarity with the poor and the weak. This is what the sign-act of the Eucharist means when we, by joining at the Table, consent to being part of Christ's Body broken, and to letting our lives be poured out for others. The church cannot enter into sign-acts without commitment to God's intention in them. The church itself *is* a sacrament to the world in acting out God's love for the world. The action of the Eucharist implies all this. It is a commitment to ethical, social, and political action as well as symbolic action—to a new kind of presence and action of the church in the world, as well as a different kind of worship. No less can be expected of a liturgy that is both praise and empowerment.

Notes

2 • THE ORIGIN OF WORSHIP IN THE GIVENNESS OF LIFE

1. Aldous Huxley, *Island* (New York: Harper & Row, 1962), p. 202.
2. Heinz Zahmt, *What Kind of God?* tr. R. A. Wilson (Minneapolis: Augsburg Press, 1971), p. 109.
3. William Golding, *Lord of the Flies* (Harmondsworth: Penguin Books, 1960), p. 51.
4. Dietrich Bonhoeffer, *Creation and Fall,* tr. J. C. Fletcher (London: SCM Press Ltd., 1959), p. 51.
5. Rudolf Bultmann, *Primitive Christianity,* tr. R. H. Fuller (New York: Meridian Books, 1956), p. 103.
6. Rudolf Otto, *The Idea of the Holy,* tr. J. W. Harvey (New York: Galaxy Press, 1958), ch. 4.
7. From Isaac Watts's hymn "When I Survey the Wondrous Cross."
8. Ernst Cassirer, *An Essay on Man* (New Haven, CT: Yale University Press, 1944), p. 108.
9. J. G. Frazer, *The Golden Bough* (London: Macmillan, 1960), p. 72.
10. Mircea Eliade, *Cosmos and History,* tr. W. R. Trask (New York: Harper Torchbooks, 1959), pp. 141ff.
11. Gerhard von Rad, *Old Testament Theology,* vol. 1, tr. D. M. G. Stalker (New York: Harper & Row, 1962), p. 218. The practice of rendering the Hebrew tetragrammaton *YHWH* as *Yahweh* will not be followed in order to retain the Hebrew sense of the divine Name as unpronounceable.
12. Eliade, p. 104.
13. Ibid.
14. Ibid., pp. 111ff.
15. Ivan Illich, *The Church, Change and Development* (New York: Herder & Herder, 1970), p. 19.
16. Northrop Frye, *The Great Code: The Bible and Literature* (Toronto: Academic Press Canada, 1982), p. 137.
17. Ibid.
18. S. Radhakrishnan, *The Bhagavadgita* (London: George Allen & Unwin Ltd., 1948), p. 158.
19. Ibid., p. 119.

20. Ibid.

21. Karl Barth, *Church Dogmatics*, vol. 2 (Edinburgh, T. & T. Clark, 1936), pp. 593ff.

22. *Gates of Prayer: The New Union Prayer Book* (New York: Central Conference of American Rabbis, 1975), p. 441.

23. Ibid., p. 419.

24. J. J. von Allmen, *Worship: Its Theology and Practice* (New York: Oxford University Press, 1965), p. 104.

25. Ferdinand Hahn, *The Worship of the Early Church*, tr. David E. Green (Philadelphia: Fortress Press, 1973), p. 80.

3 • WORSHIP IN THE NEW TESTAMENT AS A CELEBRATION OF FREEDOM

1. S. Radhakrishnan, *The Bhagavadgita* (London: George Allen & Unwin Ltd., 1948), p. 190.

2. In the Gospel of Matthew the concept of *MIKROI* "little ones" figures prominently as a designation for disciples. Cf. Matthew 11:25, 18:6.

3. John D. Crossan, *In Parables: The Challenge of the Historical Jesus* (New York: Harper & Row, 1973), p. 27.

4. Ibid., p. 32.

5. Ferdinand Hahn, *The Worship of the Early Church*, tr. David E. Green (Philadelphia: Fortress Press, 1973), p. 35.

6. Ibid., pp. 30–31.

7. Ibid., p. 106. This assertion that Christian worship is no longer cultic in nature would appear to be defining "cult" exclusively as a religious practice that takes place in a separate sacred realm and is practiced, as seen in the previous chapter with reference to the Canaanite cults, in lieu of human beings assuming responsibility for working out their own destiny in history. If the word cult is to have any application to Christian worship it will have to be used in such a way as to show the connection between ritual practice and "service by the faithful in everyday life."

8. Ibid., p. 44.

9. Ibid., p. 60.

10. Ibid., p. 71.

11. Werner Elert, *The Lord's Supper Today*, tr. M. Bertram (St. Louis: Concordia, 1973), p. 16.

12. Hahn, p. 20.

13. Ibid., p. 19.

14. Ibid., p. 25.

15. Ibid.

16. Alexander Schmemann, *Introduction to Liturgical Theology* (New York: St. Vladimir's Seminary Press, 1966), p. 47.

17. Hahn, p. 104.

18. Ibid.

19. Ibid., p. 108.

20. Ibid., pp. 71–72.

21. Ibid., p. 43.

22. Ibid., p. 105.

23. Ibid.

24. Schmemann, p. 93.

25. Ibid., p. 94.

26. See Erik H. Erikson, *Childhood and Society* (New York: W. W. Norton, 1963), p. 222.

27. J. J. von Allmen, *Worship: Its Theology and Practice* (New York: Oxford University Press, 1965).

28. Hahn, p. 106.

29. Ibid., p. 36.

30. Ibid., p. 60.

31. Ibid., p. 38.

32. Harold W. Turner, *From Temple to Meeting House: The Phenomenology and Theology of Places of Worship* (The Hague: Mouton Pub., 1979), pp. 113–14.

33. Ibid., p. 77.

34. Northrop Frye, *The Great Code: The Bible and Literature* (Toronto: Academic Press Canada, 1982), p. 29.

35. Monika K. Hellwig, *The Eucharist and the Hunger of the World* (New York: Paulist Press, 1976), p. 34.

36. Gerhard Ebeling, *Gott und Wort* (Tübingen: J. C. B. Mohr, 1966), p. 50. *"Es ist Sache des Wortes, das Nichtvorhandene, Abwesende gegenwärtig sein zu lassen." "Denn es ist Sache allein des Wortes, auch das Schlechterdings Verborgene anwesend sein zu lassen."*

37. Sallie McFague, *Metaphorical Theology* (Philadelphia: Fortress Press, 1982), p. 65. See also Susan Brooks Thistlewaite, *Metaphors for the Contemporary Church* (New York: The Pilgrim Press, 1983).

38. Crossan, p. 13.

39. McFague, p. 65.

40. Hahn does allude to a renewed application of cultic terminology metaphorically to worship in the later New Testament writings of the subapostolic age, but he regards this as a decline away from the original anticultic thrust (p. 38).

4 • FREEDOM AND AUTHORITY IN CONFLICT

1. In some of the Pauline communities women evidently were free to speak in the worship assemblies (1 Corinthians 11:5). By way of contrast, see 1 Corinthians 14:34 and 1 Timothy 2:11–12.

2. Edward Schillebeeckx, *Ministry: Leadership in the Community of Jesus Christ* (New York: Crossroad, 1981), pp. 30f.

3. The fact that "before the end of the sixth century women were forbidden to receive the bread on the naked hand" supports this interpretation. See the article on communion in *A Dictionary of Liturgy and Worship*, ed. J. G. Davies (London: SCM Press Ltd., 1972), p. 143.

4. Alexander Schmemann, *Introduction to Liturgical Theology* (New York: St. Vladimir's Seminary Press, 1966), pp. 93f.

5. T. Klauser, *A Short History of the Western Liturgy*, tr. J. Halliburton (New York: Oxford University Press, 1979), pp. 109f.

6. *St. Anselm's—Proslogion*, tr. M. J. Charlesworth (Oxford: Clarenden Press, 1965), p. 121.

7. Frederick Copleston, *A History of Philosophy*, vol. 2, pt. 2 (Garden City, NY: Doubleday, 1962), p. 65.

8. Quoted in Rudolf Bultmann, *Existence and Faith*, tr. Schubert M. Ogden (New York: Meridian Books, 1960), p. 181.

9. John Calvin, *Institutes*, vol. 1, tr. Henry Beveridge (Grand Rapids, MI: Wm. B. Eerdmans, 1962), Bk. I, p. 172.

10. Quoted by Karl Barth, *From Rousseau to Ritschl* (London: SCM Press Ltd., 1959), p. 152.

11. Immanuel Kant, *Critique of Pure Reason*, tr. N. K. Smith (London: Macmillan, 1958), p. 29.

12. Ibid., pp. 162, 174.

13. Immanuel Kant, *Religion Within the Limits of Reason Alone*, tr. T. M. Greene and H. H. Hudson (New York: Harper Torchbooks, 1960), pp. LI, LII.

14. Ibid., p. 79.

15. Ibid., pp. 187–88.

16. Ibid., p. 188.

17. Quoted by E. Fackenheim, *Metaphysics and Historicity* (Milwaukee: Marquette University Press, 1961), pp. 95–96.

18. Quoted by Fackenheim, ibid., p. 100.

19. Ludwig Feuerbach, *The Essence of Christianity* (New York: Harper Torchbooks, 1957), p. XI.

20. Ibid., p. 9.

21. Ibid., p. 26.

22. *Marx and Engels on Religion*, introduction by Reinhold Niebuhr (New York: Schocken Books, 1964), p. 42.

23. Ibid., p. 70.

24. Ibid., p. 72.

25. Feuerbach, p. XI.

5 • THE LOSS OF TRANSCENDENCE

1. Langdon Gilkey, *Naming the Whirlwind: The Renewal of God-Language* (Indianapolis: Bobbs-Merrill, 1969), p. 23.

2. Quoted by E. Fackenheim, *Metaphysics and Historicity* (Milwaukee: Marquette University Press, 1961), p. 100.

3. Henry David Thoreau, *Walden* (New York: Mentor Books, 1956), p. 71.

4. Friedrich Schleiermacher, *Religion, Speeches to Its Cultured Despisers*, tr. John Oman (New York: Harper Torchbooks, 1958), p. 39.

5. *"Schleiermachers Sendschreiben uber seine Glaubenslehre an Lucke,"* quoted by G. Ebeling in "Schleiermacher's Doctrine of the Divine Attributes" in *Journal for Theology and the Church*, ed. R. W. Funk (New York: Herder & Herder, 1970), p. 128.

6. Friedrich Schleiermacher, *The Christian Faith*, tr. D. M. Baillie; ed. H. R. Mackintosh and J. S. Stewart (New York: Harper Torchbooks, 1963), p. 17.

7. Ibid., p. 17.

8. Ibid., p. 16.

9. Ibid., p. 194.

10. Ibid., pp. 194–95.

11. Rudolf Otto, *The Idea of the Holy*, tr. J. W. Harvey (New York: Galaxy Press, 1958), pp. 10–11.

12. Ibid., p. 12.

13. Edmund Gosse, *Father and Son* (London: Landsborough Pub., 1959).

14. John Henry Newman, *Apologia Pro Vita Sua* (New York: E. P. Dutton, 1949), p. 218.

15. Ibid., p. 219.

16. This quotation is from a review of John Henry Newman's *Apologia* in *The North British Review*, August 1864, p. 46.

17. Louis Weil, *Sacraments and Liturgy* (Oxford: Basil Blackwell, 1983), p. 95.

18. Ibid.

6 • THE RECOVERY OF TRANSCENDENCE

1. Dietrich Bonhoeffer, *Letters and Papers from Prison*, ed. Eberhard Bethge (New York: Macmillan, 1972), p. 279.

2. Ibid., p. 325.

3. Ibid., p. 326.

4. Ibid., p. 327.

5. Ibid., p. 344.

6. Ibid., p. 312.

7. Ibid., p. 300.

8. Ibid., p. 370.

9. Ibid., p. 381.

10. Ibid., p. 282.

11. Dietrich Bonhoeffer, *Ethics*, tr. N. H. Smith (London: The Fontana Library, 1964), p. 196.

12. M. Novak, *Ascent of the Mountain, Flight of the Dove* (New York: Harper & Row, 1971).

13. H. Schmidt, D. Power, and H. Herder, in *Liturgy in Transition, the New Concilium* (New York: Herder & Herder, 1971), p. 11.

14. See T. Roszak, *Where the Wasteland Ends* (Garden City, NY: Doubleday, 1972).

15. Sam Keen, *To a Dancing God* (New York: Harper & Row, 1970), p. 158.

16. Ibid.

17. E. H. Maly, "The Interplay of World and Worship in the Scriptures," in *Liturgy in Transition*, p. 31.

18. Sam Keen, *Apology for Wonder* (New York: Harper & Row, 1969), p. 208.

19. Ibid., p. 209.

20. Ibid., p. 210.

21. This way of viewing anamnesis has been proposed by J. Jeremias, *The Eucharistic Words of Jesus* (Philadelphia: Fortress Press, 1966), p. 163.

22. Bonhoeffer, *Letters*, p. 300.

23. Ibid., pp. 299–300.

24. Ibid., 300.

25. Ibid.

7 • THE POWER OF METAPHOR

1. George Orwell, *1984* (Harmondsworth: Penguin Books, 1960).

2. Northrop Frye, *The Great Code: The Bible and Literature* (Toronto: Academic Press Canada, 1982), p. 7.

3. Sallie McFague, *Metaphorical Theology* (Philadelphia: Fortress Press, 1982).

4. Ibid., p. 65.

5. Martin Buber, *I and Thou*, tr. Ronald Gregor Smith (New York: Charles Scribner's Sons, 1958), p. 11.

6. McFague, p. 42.

7. Ibid., pp. 145f.

8. Ibid., p. 49.

9. "Word-event" is the language of Gerhard Ebeling. "Sign-act" is used by James F. White and others.

10. McFague, p. 14.

11. Paul Waitman Hoon suggests the use of the term transtemporalization in *The Integrity of Worship* (Nashville: Abingdon Press, 1971).

12. Emma Goldman, *Living My Life* (New York: Alfred A. Knopf, 1931), p. 56.

13. Juan L. Segundo, *The Sacraments Today*, tr. John Drury (Maryknoll, NY: Orbis Books, 1974), p. 35. Segundo is speaking of a state of "sacramental intoxication" that may require a "clearcut withdrawal" in order to enable a recovery of genuine function.

14. Ibid., p. 10.

8 • SUNDAY MORNING:
GATHERING AND SENDING FORTH

1. Gregory Dix, *The Shape of the Liturgy* (London: Dacre, 1945).

2. James F. White, *Introduction to Christian Worship* (Nashville: Abingdon Press, 1980), p. 29.

3. Marianne Micks, *The Future Present* (New York: Seabury Press, 1970), p. 21.

4. Ibid.

5. Alexander Schmemann, *Introduction to Liturgical Theology* (New York: St. Vladimir's Seminary Press, 1966), p. 77.

6. Ibid., p. 76.

7. H. Grady Davis, *Design for Preaching* (Philadelphia: Fortress Press, 1958).

8. Reuel Howe, *Partners in Preaching* (New York: Seabury Press, 1967), pp. 46f.

9. Paul Waitman Hoon, *The Integrity of Worship* (Nashville: Abingdon Press, 1971), p. 109.

10. Ibid., p. 104.

11. Robert W. Jenson, *Visible Words* (Philadelphia: Fortress Press, 1982), p. 29.

12. Edward Schillebeeckx, *Ministry: Leadership in the Community of Jesus Christ* (New York: Crossroad, 1981), p. 31.

9 • SERVICE OF THE WORD:
PROCLAMATION AND RESPONSE

1. Karl Barth, *The Word of God and the Word of Man*, tr. Douglas Horton (New York: Harper Torchbooks, 1957), pp. 28f.

2. Juan Luis Segundo, *The Liberation of Theology* (Maryknoll, NY: Orbis Books, 1976), p. 9.

3. R. Funk, *Language, Hermeneutic, and the Word of God* (New York: Harper & Row, 1966), p. 127.

4. Gerhard Ebeling, *Word and Faith*, tr. James W. Leitch (London: SCM Press Ltd., 1963), p. 331.

5. Karl Barth, *Prayer and Preaching* (London: SCM Press Ltd., 1964), p. 112.

6. Karl Barth, *Church Dogmatics*, vol. I, 1, tr. G. T. Thomson (Edinburgh: T & T Clark, 1936), p. 45.

7. Fred Craddock, *As One Without Authority* (Nashville: Abingdon Press, 1979).

8. John D. Crossan, *In Parables: The Challenge of the Historical Jesus* (New York: Harper & Row, 1973), p. 13.

9. Quoted by H. G. Stuempfle Jr., *Preaching Law and Gospel* (Philadelphia: Fortress Press, 1978), p. 25.

10. Ebeling, p. 281.

11. Ibid., p. 278.

12. Stuempfle, p. 25.

13. Ibid., p. 22.

14. Jurgen Moltmann, *The Crucified God*, tr. R. A. Wilson and John Bowden (London: SCM Press Ltd., 1974), p. 186.

15. Gerhard Ebeling, *Luther: An Introduction to His Thought* (Philadelphia: Fortress Press, 1970), pp. 116f.

16. Dietrich Bonhoeffer, in *Ethics*, tr. N. H. Smith (London: The Fontana Library, 1964), pp. 305–6, writes: "The *tertius usus* defines the law as God's merciful help in the performance of the works which are commanded."

17. Barth, *Church Dogmatics*.

18. Gerhard Ebeling, *The Nature of Faith*, tr. R. G. Smith (London: The Fontana Library, 1966). Chapter 2 in Ebeling's book is entitled "The Witness of Faith" as a way of referring to the Jesus of history.

19. Leander Keck, *The Bible in the Pulpit* (Nashville: Abingdon Press, 1978), p. 138.

20. P. T. Forsyth, *Positive Preaching and the Modern Mind* (London: Independent Press, 1957), p. 62.

158

1. James F. White, *Sacraments as God's Self-giving* (Nashville: Abingdon Press, 1983).

2. *The Last Supper;* directed by Tomas Gutierrez Alea. Produced in 1976 by the Instituto Cubano del Arte e Industria Cinematograficos.

3. White, p. 30.

4. Paul Ricoeur, *The Symbolism of Evil*, tr. E. Buchanan (New York: Harper & Row, 1967), p. 165.

5. Quoted by Robert Jenson, *Visible Words* (Philadelphia: Fortress Press, 1982), p. 3.

6. Ricoeur, p. 45.

7. G. Gutierrez, *A Theology of Liberation* (Maryknoll, NY: Orbis Books, 1973), pp. 258f.